A HEAD
FULL OF BLUE

NICK JOHNSTONE

BLOOMSBURY

First published in Great Britain 2002
This paperback edition published 2003

Copyright © 2002 by Nick Johnstone

Grateful acknowledgement is made to the following for permission
to reprint excerpts from previously published material:

The Bell Jar by Sylvia Plath
Reproduced by permission of the Estate of Sylvia Plath and Faber and Faber Ltd.

'Cut' from *Collected Poems* by Sylvia Plath
Reproduced by permission of the Estate of Sylvia Plath and Faber and Faber Ltd.

'Gravy' from *All of Us: The Collected Poems of Raymond Carver*
by Raymond Carver
© Tess Gallagher 1996. Reproduced by permission of the Estate of
Raymond Carver c/o Rogers, Coleridge and White Ltd., 20 Powis Mews,
London W11 1JN in association with International Creative Management.

The Twelve Steps of Alcoholics Anonymous
© 1939 AA World Services Inc. Reprinted with permission.

'Are you an Alcoholic?' questionnaire from test questions as used by the
Johns Hopkins Bayview Medical Center, Baltimore, Maryland. Reprinted with
permission of Johns Hopkins Bayview Medical Center, Baltimore, Maryland.

The moral right of the author has been asserted

Bloomsbury Publishing Plc, 38 Soho Square, London W1D 3HB

A CIP catalogue record is
available from the British Library

ISBN 0 7475 6170 2

Typeset by Hewer Text Ltd, Edinburgh
Printed in Great Britain by Clays Ltd, St Ives Plc

For Anna

ACKNOWLEDGEMENTS

Special thanks to Alexandra Pringle for editing this book so intuitively and with such care, for making editorial suggestions that also had an impact on my real life, for helping me to see what I couldn't see, for teaching me so much about writing and for being so kind and supportive. Thanks to Hannah Griffiths at Curtis Brown for being both a good friend and a wonderful agent. Thanks to Tanja Howarth for finding this book a good home, and to Matthew Hamilton, David Reynolds, Minna Fry and Katie Collins for believing in it from the beginning, to Pascal Cariss for his keen eye during the final editing stages, to Chiki Sarkar and Marian McCarthy for seeing it all through and to everyone else at Bloomsbury for investing so much passion in this book. Big hug to Anya Rosenberg for taking this book to heart, working miracles and our music trivia chats. Tip of the hat to Tim Hyde and Sean Body for early feedback and to Allan Jones for giving me the space to work through my stuff. April Magnuson: I know you know. I'm indebted to Paul Westerberg for the words of wisdom and for showing me the way. Love to my family. Lastly, this book is dedicated to the memory of MN who never got to read it.

PART ONE

1

When I was fourteen, I got drunk for the first time. Champagne drunk. My mouth was stretched in a smile so wide that my jaw hurt. The sky had the colours of a bruise. It was October 1984. Freezing cold and depressing. I was at my cousin's eighteenth birthday party. Her step-father pointed a champagne bottle towards me like a loaded gun. I watched the bubbles pirouette in the glass. The champagne picked through my brain like an electrician. Faulty circuits were re-wired. Loose cables were soldered. When the repairs were complete, my eyes sang as beautifully as Billie Holiday.

2

People always ask, Why did you stop drinking? They never ask, Why did you start drinking? Just like people always want to know why you broke up with someone before they want to know how you fell in love with them in the first place. I suppose there's some comfort to be had in other peoples' suffering. I never have any black-and-white answers. All I can tell them is that there was no champagne when I stopped drinking, only pain.

No one I have ever met – outside Alcoholics Anonymous meetings that is – remembers the first time they got drunk quite as romantically as I do. For me, that night was an epiphany. Nothing would ever be the same again. I found a cure for the humming in my head. That nameless, shapeless humming. And once I knew it didn't have to be there, my response was only natural: I wanted to stay cured.

When I was eleven the humming got louder. It was no longer a single wasp, trapped inside my skull. There were many wasps, bees too, all humming until there was an itch inside my brain, an exhausting itch I had no hope of scratching. The humming wanted to take centre-stage so it threw a tantrum one morning when my mother was driving me to school. I'd recently given up smiling. I was in training for all the other things I'd later give up. My mother pulled up to the kerb outside the gates. What's the matter? she asked. You seem so fed up at the moment. Hum. Buzz. I don't know, I said. This was to be my mantra for the next fifteen years: I don't know. We talked a little about why I hated school and why I seemed so sad all the time. There were no tidy summaries though, no precise sentences prefaced by 'I feel'. When I opened the door, the humming was so loud I couldn't hear her say goodbye, I could only read her lips.

My childhood up to this point was fairly typical. We lived in Surrey until I was ten and life there was much the same as life for any other middle-class family growing up close to London in the 1970s. My mother stopped working when she became pregnant with me and stayed home to raise first me and then my sister, who was born when I was four. My father worked hard, always leaving before my sister and I woke up and coming home long after we were in bed. We spent week nights doing homework and week-ends staying with or visiting grandparents and other family.

The rest of the time we had TV and Rolling Stones records and a paddling pool in the back garden in summer and prayers at bed-time and scary masks for Halloween and fireworks for Guy Fawkes' Night and swimming lessons during school holidays and sand-castles on the beach and homework and ice cream and Sunday after-noons in winter wrapped in blankets on the living room floor watching Pink Panther films.

My parents tell me I was a quiet and withdrawn child, at my happiest hidden away in the corner of a room, writing a story or drawing a picture. I never really had any friends – I wasn't interested – and lived mostly inside my head. Without the distractions of others, I did well at school, often coming top of my classes. In December 1980, we left Surrey and moved to a new house in Buckinghamshire, some twenty-five miles from Central London. A year later, I passed the eleven-plus exam and got into a local gram-mar school. And then, when I was eleven, this humming, humid and close.

Had you noticed it before? a therapist would later ask. Not with such clarity, I told her. But I had known from an early age that there was something different about me, that something sinister lingered in the shadows of my everyday, that a dolorous shimmer glowed about me, that the company I kept was a reflection of the way I felt. This *something else* was there when I came home crying because a classmate at school told me his mother had died by choking on a piece of bacon rind; it was there when I befriended a girl at primary school who had five fingers missing; it was there in the hours I spent obsessing about the young sad-faced neighbour whose husband had died in a plane crash; it was there when I was eight and became close friends with a boy from a school whom no one would talk to because he had to wear callipers on his legs; it was there when I wouldn't ride my bicycle beyond a certain speed because I thought it would give me a heart attack; it was there when I broke down on the stairs one Saturday morning because I thought the world was going to be destroyed by nuclear war. The therapist nodded. So it was there from the beginning, she said. Yes, I said. I suppose it was.

6

When I was seven, I started to talk in my sleep, grind my teeth and sleepwalk. My parents would find me muttering nonsense to a wardrobe or trying to open a window that didn't exist. Once, I hid behind my bedroom door and jumped out on my father when he came looking for the source of the banging and crashing sounds that had woken both him and my mother up. Another time, on a family summer holiday in Tenerife, I was shaken out of a sleep-walking trance by strangers. Somehow, almost naked, I had got out of bed and walked to the other side of the hotel.

7

When I got a bad report card for Maths, my mother made me a giant times table chart which she hung on my bedroom wall. We practised sums at bed-time. My favourite was eight times eight equals sixty-four. Later, I would tell people that drinking was like multiplying the slopes and curves of eight times eight, getting drunk the glorious answer: sixty-four.

8

It was a hot, sunny day in May or June 1984. School was lazy, quiet. The exams were over and I, like everyone else, was looking forward to the end of the summer term. It was mid-morning. Break was on. I was talking with a friend out on the playing fields. He said he was thirsty. I said I craved a freezing-cold glass of Coca-Cola. He gave me an odd look. I drank two or three glasses every night. My mother bought big plastic bottles from the supermarket. I'd come in from school, get my homework done, take a bath and then head to the refrigerator. It was my favourite part of each day. I loved to watch the door swing open and there it would be: a two-litre bottle of Coke shivering in the bottle rack. When I poured some into a glass, the bubbles fizzed, and if it was a hot day, the icy liquid would let out a hiss when it collided with room temperature. I'd grab a packet of crisps and settle down in front of the TV. When the first sip hit the back of my throat, the craving stopped. So there I was, standing out on the school fields in the middle of a summer morning, my throat aching because I wanted that first sip of chilled Coca-Cola. I was about to turn fourteen, the sun was too bright.

9

After getting that drunk at my cousin's eighteenth party, my parents rarely allowed me to drink any alcohol. They let me have a small glass of wine with Sunday lunch when we saw grandparents and they also let me have a small glass on special occasions such as a birthday or Easter or Christmas. It was never enough though and I remember how my throat always drooled, how one glass was never anything but a tease. How the tiny flash of not feeling like myself was so incredible, so miraculous, that I'd stare at the empty glass and dream of a day when I could feel like that all the time.

10

When I was fifteen, sixteen, seventeen, Sylvia Plath's *The Bell Jar* was my bible. I used to be able to quote entire passages, my memory word-drunk on the effervescence of her writing. I read and re-read that book. My head foggy with teenage fantasies, I dreamed of falling in love with a girl like Esther Greenwood. We would cling to each other like sticky death wishes, brush our blue-grey lips together, make suicide pacts. Sometimes, late at night, alone in bed, I would put the book down and wonder what was wrong with me.

11

In autumn 1986, a man who lived across the street from us died of bowel cancer. He was in his early thirties, had a Swiss wife and two little daughters who liked to chase each other around the front lawn. I came home from school one day and broke down crying at the kitchen table. My mother was fixing me a cup of tea and a slice of toast. I was staring at the patterns on the wooden table. I'd never noticed how the grain of the wood swirled, sometimes breaking into a spiral, sometimes ordered and curled like a question mark. What's wrong? she asked. I can't stop thinking about the neighbour. But you didn't even know him. That's not the point, I said. What is the point then? I don't know, I said and covered my face with my hands.

12

It was on the school bus that I came to know Ben and Paul who were both in the same year as me. They lived six doors apart on a street that ran parallel to mine. We had no great common bond but routine brought us together and eventually we became close friends. Ben was cautious, conservative. He was raised in a Catholic home, crucifixes and portraits of the Virgin Mary hung everywhere. His dream was to become a doctor. Years later, he'd move back to his mother's native Poland and set up practice. Paul was intense, always bristling with too much energy, always making more plans than there was time. His parents had recently separated and he was doing a good job of hiding just how painful it was for him. But we knew. He was the first of us to start smoking. He was also the one who initiated trips – two, three nights a week – to the pub opposite our bus stop.

13

Sixteen years old and munching on the early days of our A-level courses, we were typical teenagers, arguing with our parents, nursing crushes on unobtainable older girls, smoking on the school bus and getting drunk at the only pub that didn't ask us for ID. We often turned up to school hung over, stumbled off the bus and rushed into town in search of cigarettes before the first class of the day. We pooled loose change from our Saturday jobs and tried a different brand every day: Camel, Salem, Reyno, Consulate, Dunhill, Gauloises, Peter Stuyvesant, Marlboro, Kent, Winston, Parliament . . . We smoked our way through them all like we'd been hired as a focus group by some marketing guru. And then, on days when we had no money to buy cigarettes – a cause of arguments on the bus – I began to see there was beautiful order in addiction.

Robert and I became friends because we shared the same birthday – 11 June – had pretty much the same record collections and both played guitar. We had taken to jamming in each other's bedroom at the weekends. Every Tuesday night, for reasons I now forget, we bought bottles of wine and cans of beer and headed to some nearby deserted woods. There, we drank and smoked and talked about music. One particular night, I was in a wretched mood. Fever-pitch humming had me desperate to flee myself. I bought two bottles of white wine. Robert bought one. Once we found a good spot, I opened my first bottle and drank it down in one, no pausing for air, the glug glug of the vanishing wine pulsating in my ears. When it was empty, I threw the bottle out into the darkness.

'Better?' Robert said, and laughed.

On our way there, probably to make up for my lack of conversation, he told me how he had crushed an aspirin tablet on to his parents' kitchen table before coming out and then snorted it using a five-pound note. When I asked why, he said he was practising for the day when he could get some cocaine.

'Yes,' I said. 'Pass me the corkscrew will you?'

'Show off,' he said and threw it at me. 'Who do you think you are? Keith Richards?'

Robert had taken no more than two sips of his wine. I popped the cork out of bottle number two.

Later, when the second bottle was empty, I was running around in the dark, a Gitanes hanging from my lips, when I lost my footing and fell down a steep slope, tumbling and spinning, until I came to a stop in a thicket of bramble bushes.

Robert had to walk me home. My mother exploded when she saw how drunk I was. She saw me up to bed and then drove Robert to his house. He said she grilled him all the way, asking questions like, Why on earth does Nick have to get that drunk?

The next morning, I had to go to the school nurse and have dozens of thorns tweezered out of my arms and legs.

15

Robert and I started to jam at the weekends with Paul (who played bass) and a friend of his called Dennis (whom Robert and I vaguely knew from school) on drums. We got along well and it took no more than a few rehearsals for us to consider ourselves not only a band but friends too. We made our live debut at a party thrown by someone who knew someone whose parents were away. We arrived at this house in the afternoon and got drunk as soon as we had set up our equipment. By the time the house was filled with a hundred plus fifteen-year-olds, we were too drunk to even tune our instruments, let alone play them. After thirty minutes of trying and failing to play 'Louie, Louie', someone cut the power. Our amps coughed and packed up. We tossed our instruments down in disgust. It was Dennis's idea that we go upstairs. Why? Robert asked. So we can trash the place, deadpanned Dennis. He led us into a bedroom and opened all the windows. Then he locked the door and began to pull out drawers – filled with socks, underwear, letters, cassettes – and empty them out the windows. We joined in. After an hour, the trees and bushes and flowers below were strewn with the contents of the bedroom. Then, we went down-stairs, packed up our gear and left.

16

Ben's parents were in Poland for a fortnight so he invited me over to his house to split a litre of high-strength Polish vodka.

'I want you home by eleven,' my father said as I tied my shoe laces. 'It's a school night.'

'I will be,' I said. 'Don't worry about it.'

Ben and I walked to the local off-licence to buy a mixer. I chose a bottle of sparkling wine.

'Are you serious?' Ben said. 'It'll be a lethal combination.'

'That's the point you idiot,' I said and took it to the counter.

When we had drunk the litre of vodka and all of the sparkling wine, I got up to change the TV channel and passed out stone-cold on the carpet. Apparently, Ben spent several minutes trying to revive me before he passed out too. When we both came round, we crawled to the toilet and lay side by side, taking turns to throw up. When I managed to stay upright long enough to consider walking home, I staggered off down the street, ricocheting off hedgerows and street signs. I saw a figure in the darkness coming towards me. It was my father. It was after 1.30 am. He said that he and my mother couldn't sleep, that they were worried sick about me. Why was I so drunk? What the hell did I think I was playing at?

The band was a novelty that soon wore off. When we stopped rehearsing, nobody cared except Paul. His insistence that we keep playing was to the rest of us nothing but another symptom of how badly he was dealing with his parents' separation. We tried to get him to talk about it but he refused. And the less he talked about it, the more agitated he got about everything else. He started to smoke a lot of pot before, during and after school, and took to watching the kinds of sci-fi movies that only make sense if you're stoned. He went off the rails – as far as we were concerned – when he fell in love with Suzy, a girl who spent all her time at the community Baptist church. A few dates with her and Paul was a committed Baptist. His overnight embracing of religion got up our noses, including Ben's, who was offended that Paul had chosen the Baptist faith over Catholicism. We made fun of Paul, offering to baptise him with our pints of beer. It took him several minutes to get the joke, because even though he was now a Baptist, he was also a very stoned Baptist.

One day, Paul's tutor at school burst into my History class and asked if he could speak to me in private. I went outside with him. 'Paul's gone missing,' he said. 'His mother thinks you might know where he is.' I didn't. A week later the police brought him home. It transpired that he had cleaned out his savings account and fled to Birmingham with Suzy. When they were back, Suzy broke up with him and then it was over, his little fantasy where they went on the run like lovers in a Nicholas Ray movie.

In October 1987 I met Katherine at a party. When I first saw her she was dancing to 'Love Will Tear Us Apart' by Joy Division. I had no nose for omens in those days so I crossed the room and decided to fall in love with her. She had Marilyn Monroe hips and a nervous, shrill laugh. We started going out, mostly to pubs after our first date – a stolen afternoon at a coffee shop during school hours – had turned into a disaster. Sober, I came across as a rambling Woody Allen, a mumbling Marlon Brando, knocked a cup of coffee all over the table and made a fool of myself.

Three weeks into our 'relationship' – and to be honest, it would be more accurate to say that we happened to be in the same room from time to time – I offered to drive to a big party that someone from school was having the following weekend at a nearby night club. 'Oh don't drive,' she said. 'You're such fun when you're drunk.'

So I didn't drive to the party . . . instead I drank before I went out and I drank on the way to the club and when I got there, already on my way to being drunk, I found Katherine at the first-floor bar wearing a yellow dress with a faded denim jacket draped across her shoulders. Her lipstick was blood-red, her neck pale as Russia. No matter what I said she didn't seem to give a damn. Things that usually made her laugh didn't, things that she liked to talk about failed to raise a spark of interest either. We were icy strangers, her cheekbones blue with indifference.

The music was deafening. On the matt-black dance floor, strobe lights licked the lips of young lovers. She dragged me by the sleeve of my jacket to an upstairs corridor, bare brick walls chaperoning us, a scuffed cigarette machine the only witness to her short, sharp breaking-up speech. Her lipstick sprang into action fast, framing every sentence with a red O. There was no, I Love You, just a curt: I'm sorry but this isn't working.

I went to the second floor, spilled into a crowd of strangers, pushed to the bar. Held hostage by a flurry of adolescent hormones, I was about to act as though I'd been brutally abandoned by the love of my life, rather than dumped by someone who was more 'girl' and 'friend' than girlfriend. My reaction – and the makers of *Dawson's Creek* couldn't have scripted it any better – had nothing whatsoever to do with her.

I ordered a double Scotch. I downed it in one go and ordered another before the change from the first drink had even stopped rattling on the counter. I downed that and ordered a third. When I downed that too, the bartender refused to serve me again. I headed for the first floor. My thoughts were ice cubes playing a cello. The Scotch was screaming in my veins. I pushed through webs of restless elbows until I saw Katherine: her mouth breaking into a smile, her shoulders rising and falling as she laughed, a cigarette dangling from her fingers. For a second I stepped out of the moment and was someone else, examining the scene I had just stumbled into. She looked so happy. What a smile . . .

I locked myself in a toilet cubicle. I took off my belt and wrapped it around my neck. I pulled the belt as tight as it would go. There was a wonderful hush. It was quite nice for a few seconds, like a daydream or having your photograph taken, but then consciousness started to drift away. I considered my options but common sense took hold of the situation and had me release my grip. The belt fell to the floor. The buckle rattled when it hit the tiles. The strip lights were too bright. I returned to life, my chest heaving, my teeth chewing on handfuls of spiky oxygen. I spluttered several times, spun round and vomited into the toilet.

19

We got to the cinema early and, after buying tickets, sat on some steps. My mouth watered when I thought of a gin and tonic trickling over a nest of ice cubes. I was sure that she was wondering where the other 'me' was, the one that had kissed her at a party the previous Saturday and asked her out on this date.

'What's the matter?' she said after another few minutes of awkward silence.

'My last girlfriend – the one I was telling you about – thought I was only fun when I was drunk.'

People buzzed around us, hurrying to other films showing at the multiplex.

'Don't be silly,' she said, putting two and two together. 'I like you just as you are.'

Her voice was soft and reassuring, her long brown hair a place to fall asleep in and never wake up.

'Really?'

A smile lit up her face. I told her that I'd driven because I didn't want to pretend to be something I wasn't. She put her hand on my leg.

'It's OK,' she said. 'Really. Don't worry.'

She leaned over and gave me a kiss on the cheek.

'Come on,' she said. 'The film's about to begin.'

On the way back from the cinema, I could hear the stiffness in my voice as I said one stupid thing after another about the film. She didn't say much so I gave up after a while and turned Sonic Youth up. When we got close to our homes, which were five minutes' walk from each other, I suggested that we dump my mother's car and wander up to the pub for a drink.

'Why?' she asked, as I pulled into my parents' driveway.

'Oh you mean after what I said earlier?'

I turned the engine off, knowing that I was minutes away from a drink curing me of all awkwardness.

'I don't want you to think that you have to have a drink to impress me.'

'I don't,' I lied. 'It would just be fun. That's all.'

20

Elizabeth and I were together for the next two years. It was perhaps her shyness that made her beautiful to me. She was such a gentle person. Idealistic too. She believed she could change the world. Aside from being a vegetarian, she belonged to Greenpeace, anti-apartheid groups, animal rights groups, CND, Amnesty International. She was precociously well read and ranked Camus and J.D. Salinger as her favourite writers. She always wore vintage dresses and Doctor Marten boots. Smoked Marlboro Lights. Drank Scotch. She modelled herself on Andy Warhol superstar Edie Sedgwick, using Jean Stein's biography – which she stole from the library – as her guide to life. A year into our relationship, she cut her hair short like Edie and took to wearing thick, black rings of kohl around her eyes. The other copycat accessories, such as amphetamines and eating disorders, were to come much later.

Our relationship was obsessive and intense from the start. We quickly came to hate being apart for any amount of time, seeing school and our Saturday jobs – she worked in a chemist's, I worked in the local library – as enemies to our intimacy. When homework kept us home working, we'd speak on the phone until our parents yelled at us to get off the line. The rest of the time, we went out whenever we could, bingeing on each other's company, revelling in our exile, happy with the solitude of a kiss. There was a downside to this love, though, too much passion sometimes tipping us out of balance. On nights when she wouldn't say a word and sat crying in the car as we drove around poorly lit streets and lanes, I wondered if she was my Esther Greenwood, my blue-lipped girl, my embalmed twin.

21

Nights at the pub, with friends, with Elizabeth, were trips to a parallel universe. When I walked through the doors of a pub, I walked back into time before life, into the womb. When I rested my elbows on the bar, I was home, everything that was wrong in my life left out in the cold, pawing at the doors. When I had that first drink inside me, I was immune to everything. There was nothing, nothing in the whole wide world, that could touch me.

22

We were making the long walk home after a night's drinking with friends at a far-flung pub. There was a storm brewing between us. The humidity of our silence was making my hair curl. I wanted her to just come out and say them, the words that popped up like burnt toast whenever I pushed things too far. I was in a down mood. I'd just made a mess of my mock A levels – barely passing English and failing History and Politics. Everyone was on my case: my parents, my sister, Elizabeth, teachers, the school.

'I wish you'd stop drinking so much.'

There it was. Right on cue.

'Oh Jesus. Just drop it.'

The space between us was heavy, swollen. How do you tell someone who loves you that there's this thing that makes you feel better than they ever could?

'It's scaring me,' she said and she meant it, her eyes were full of fear. 'I don't like it when you get drunk and make everyone laugh and they think you're fun to be with. And the minute we leave the pub, your mood changes and you're miserable again.'

I went to put my arm around her – perhaps hoping to shut her up – but she pushed me away.

'And another thing,' she added. 'I'm sick of all our dates revolving around drinking.'

I paused to light a cigarette. For a second she sailed ahead of me. I thought of letting her go. She stopped and turned around to face me.

'It's not that bad,' I said.

'It is from where I'm standing.'

'And what if it makes me feel good?'

'That's crap and you know it.'

'No it's not. It turns me into someone else. Someone I like.'

'Why can't you just be yourself?'

Her question rang out over all the houses that were in darkness, the trees that were still, the clouds overhead that were passing in slow motion.

23

School was over. The A-level exam results were out. I got better grades than anyone expected. I blew off my offer of a place to study American Literature at the University of East Anglia because I didn't want to be away from Elizabeth. Instead, I decided to take a gap year and reapply to study English at the University of London. In the meantime, as I'd done all summer long, I worked four days a week at the library. One Saturday, there was a book sale. I turned up with a massive hangover and was asked to make sure that every book on the sale trolley was priced before the doors opened to the public. I sipped a mug of black coffee while I sifted through the books. One of them – *Alcoholism and the Facts* – caught my eye and I pulled it from the stack. There was a questionnaire on the back cover headed 'Are You An Alcoholic?'. I hurried through each question, answering yes or no.

1 Do you lose time from work due to drinking?
  No.
2 Is drinking making your home life unhappy?
  No.
3 Do you drink because you are shy with other people?
  Yes.

4 Is drinking affecting your reputation?
Yes.

5 Have you ever felt remorse after drinking?
Yes.

6 Have you ever gotten into financial difficulties as a result of drinking?
No.

7 Do you turn to lower companions and an inferior environment when drinking?
No.

8 Does your drinking make you careless of your family's welfare?
No.

9 Has your ambition decreased since drinking?
Yes.

10 Do you crave a drink at a definite time daily?
Yes.

11 Do you want a drink the next morning?
No.

12 Does drinking cause you to have difficulty sleeping?
Yes.

13 Has your efficiency decreased since drinking?
Yes.

14 Is drinking jeopardising your job or business?
No.

15 Do you drink to escape from worries or trouble?
Yes.

16 Do you drink alone?
No.

17 Have you ever had a complete loss of memory as a result of drinking?
No.

18 Has your physician ever treated you for drinking?
   No.
19 Do you drink to build up your self-confidence?
   Yes.
20 Have you ever been to a hospital or institution on account of drinking?
   No.

I answered *Yes* to nine of the twenty questions. I was relieved and about to put the book back on the sale trolley when I saw the foot-note at the end of the questionnaire: 'If you have answered YES to any one of the questions, there is a definite warning that you may be alcoholic. If you have answered YES to any two, the chances are that you are an alcoholic. If you have answered YES to three or more, you are definitely an alcoholic.' I stuffed the book back on the trolley and went back to checking the rest of the books. When my break came, I went over to the trolley and hid the book in the geography section. Whenever there was a sale, members of staff were allowed to take home any books that were left at the end of the day. When the doors were closed to the public, I slipped the book inside my jacket and took it home. I stuffed it in a drawer and never read a page. Until years later of course, when I needed to.

24

'This is creepy,' said Elizabeth. 'I don't think we're going to find it.'

We stood with our hands on our hips, wondering if we wanted to carry on checking the graves. There were so many that we hadn't looked at. The sky was turning blacker.

'Find her,' I corrected. 'I don't think we're going to find her.'

The day before, Elizabeth and I had driven to Leeds to see Bruce Springsteen. We stayed the night with her grandmother and then took a detour the following afternoon to find Sylvia Plath's grave.

'Should we just go?' she said.

A lot of the graves were laid on a steep slope which was difficult to walk down.

'Let's look one last time. Down there.'

'Do we have to?'

'Yes.'

'What's the point?'

I was already edging my way down. I could hear her groaning but I kept on, checking one name after another. Elizabeth clambered down and stood beside me.

'Please tell me why we're doing this,' she said. 'I need to know.'

I knew her well enough to know she was going to cry.

'We're doing this so that she lives on.'

'But her books do that.'

'I want more than just the books,' I said. 'I want to tell her what *The Bell Jar* means to me.'

She held out her hand, palm up. I felt it too. Drops of rain.

'I think she already knows.'

I moved backwards, so I could see one last grave. It wasn't hers. The epitaph read: *Even In The Midst Of Life, We Are In Death*.

'Look at this,' I said. 'It's beautiful.'

She climbed down.

When we got back to the car, we were soaked.

25

I got a job working in an off-licence. A lot of drinking went on in there. It was the manager's doing. He didn't care about anything. He slipped bottles of Moët et Chandon and Lanson Black Label into his bag at the end of each day. He used to encourage us to drink during the day, saying things like, Put this new Japanese beer in the refrigerator. I want you all to sample it this afternoon. Twice a week, we all had to work a 9am to 9pm shift. I was always put on with Mark, the biggest drinker on staff. We'd open the doors at 9am and at 9.15 he'd chuck a can of beer over to me and we'd start drinking. This went on all day – we had to match each other drink for drink – and by mid-afternoon we'd be ripped out of our minds. One night, when he was too drunk to serve a customer, he abandoned the counter and locked himself in the stock room. He sent me out to serve her while his hysterical laughter rang out around the shop. She asked me what was wrong with him. I told her he was working too hard. Oh, she said and handed me her credit card.

26

My parents bought a new house three miles away from our old one which meant that I could no longer walk over to see Elizabeth. At the same time, all of my friends scattered. Dennis was at university. Ben, Paul and Robert were away cramming for re-takes after failing their A levels. My mood was a see-saw, tipping this way and that. There was continuous turbulence. All summer long, I bought fourpacks of beer and kept them in the refrigerator. Colt 45. Miller Lite. Coors. Budweiser. Icepacks that numbed my thoughts. Now, my hands cold with the onset of winter, I ate dinner with my parents and sister and then drove over to see Elizabeth. We'd hang out for an hour or two and then I'd head home and settle in my bedroom with my chilled cans of beer and write poems about the humming that was driving me crazy.

27

In November 1988, I went for an interview at Goldsmiths' College, University of London. The Head of the English department asked me, 'What do you think of Shakespeare?'

With all the snottiness of youth, I said, 'I'd take a Bob Dylan album over the complete works of Shakespeare any day.'

He offered me a place there and then, before we had even talked about the course, my background, writers, writing. I went home and celebrated by getting drunk.

28

'Where did you get that from?'

He smirked. His hands were full of five-pound notes,

ten-pound notes. We were hospital porters. I had left the off-licence and was now working as a temp, going from one job to another.

'Nurses.'

I stared again at the money and then back at his face.

'What do you mean?'

We were on our break, sitting in the hospital staff room, waiting for the intercom to call us to take a patient somewhere or to go into an operating theatre and turn a patient over.

'How do you think they make it through their night shifts?'

I thought about it. Some of the nurses always looked terrible – pale with charcoal-grey half-moons beneath bloodshot eyes.

'What are you saying?'

He had five earrings in his left ear. His head was shaved. His tattoos contracted every time he rubbed the stubble on his skull.

'Speed,' he whispered. 'I supply the nurses.'

'You're dealing speed in here?'

He laughed. My naiveté embarrassed me.

'Do you want some?'

I shook my head.

'Goody two shoes,' he said.

The intercom summoned us to one of the operating theatres. When we got there, there was blood everywhere, on the walls, on the floor, on the gurney. I couldn't stand the sight of blood.

Two weeks later, I quit that job too.

'I don't want that,' she said.

Elizabeth and I were sitting in her bedroom. Morrissey was whining about something on her tinny stereo. She was sick with glandular fever. My short career as a temp was already history. I was now working at a local health foods store.

'Want what?'

I was still going over to see her almost every night. She'd fix me a brandy as soon as I walked through the front door.

'You kissing me.'

'What's that supposed to mean?'

We had been arguing ever since I left school. It seemed as though my gap year was wrecking everything. That and the glandular fever.

'You know.'

She stared at my left foot. I looked down. I was crushing her dog-eared copy of J.D. Salinger's *Franny And Zooey*. I pushed it out the way.

'What? You don't find me attractive any more?'

'I don't know.'

I looked down at my drink for support. It was empty. She looked at me, doe eyes, apologetic smile, hands clasped, barefoot, snow-white legs, the hem of her skirt riding high.

'What do you mean you don't know?'

'I just don't know if I feel that way about you any more.'

Her mother was shouting about something downstairs. Morrissey had nothing more to say. The tape had ended. Silence took over the room like a bad smell.

Something wasn't right because my eyes wouldn't open – something was making them stick together. My head was so thick with the vodka from the night before that it took me a while to figure out what was happening. After arguing with Elizabeth, I stopped off on the way home for a bottle of vodka and a cheap mixer. Everyone was asleep when I got in so I drank the vodka slumped in front of the TV. I remember the screen getting blurry and then – the next thing I knew – my mother put a cup of tea beside my bed and drew the curtains. My eyelids – like windscreen wipers struggling to clear cold, sticky porridge from my eyeballs – opened. The duvet cover was damp and cold. My mother came back into my bedroom with a puzzled look on her face. What's that smell? I sat up fast and the stench choked me. There was vomit over bed covers, up the bedroom wall, over the carpet, in my hair, over my face and chest and arms. What have you done! she screamed. I had thrown up in my sleep . . .

Forty-five minutes later I was behind the counter at the health foods store, trying to answer customers' questions about vitamins and supplements. I lasted no more than fifteen minutes before having to rush to the staff toilet to puke again. The owner of the store sent me home. I told him it was a bug. The next day, man to boy in the warehouse, he asked me if I was feeling better. I said I was. He gave me a knowing smile and handed me a bag of oats saying, I guess you had a bit too much to drink didn't you? I didn't say anything and carried the bag of oats over to the store, the coarse fabric of the sack rubbing against my sweating hands.

'We shouldn't see each other for a while.'

It took a mere ten syllables for Elizabeth to put a bullet through the head of fourteen months of love.

'Can I call you?' I pleaded.

She shook her head. No matter how often she wiped her face, there were more tears.

'This sounds like the end. Is it the end for us?'

She shook her head again. I stood up. I put my jacket on.

'I love you,' I said and left her sitting on her bed.

32

Late at night, when I was alone and drunk, thoughts flickered in my rotting brain: driving off a cliff, hanging myself from a tree, running a hot bath and slashing my wrists, jumping off a tall building, sitting in the garage with my car running, cutting my throat with a carving knife. Everywhere I went, I saw new ways, new possibilities. Lamp-posts. Motorway bridges. Building sites. Plastic containers marked 'poison'. This was all I looked for. I had a black smile, ugly pinpricks spun beneath the shade of my eyelids. I was dreaming of peace of mind or, better still, a mouth filled with moist soil. I spoke through my ears, listened through my nostrils, breathed through my hair. There was nonsense in the air and my hands were utterly, completely empty.

One Monday morning, I woke up and didn't want to get out of bed. All I wanted was to go back to sleep. I liked it there in the land of sleep. Pillow, bed, duvet. It was so simple. Mid-morning, I was sent across the road from the health foods store to make up snack bags of nuts and grains. The warehouse was cold and cramped and there were no windows. I was cutting pieces of tape with a Stanley knife. It was store policy to seal the bags with one piece of vertically applied tape. I stopped what I was doing. I picked up the knife and stroked the tip of the blade across the top of my thumb. *What a thrill. My thumb instead of an onion. The top quite gone. Except for a sort of a hinge. Of skin. A flap like a hat. Dead white. Then that red plush*. The blade left a white line. All the air was sucked out of that warehouse. The blade was holding its breath. We were both afraid. I rolled my shirt sleeve up. My veins were hiding. I saw pools of blood and flashing blue lights as I held the blade, in my shaking hand, just millimetres above those shivering veins. I was ready to step out of this life when the warehouse door swung open and daylight shocked me.

'OK, Nick? How are the bags coming along?'

It was the owner. He was in his late fifties, always positive, always keen. I put the knife down.

'Fine,' I said. 'Everything's just fine.'

34

When the humming eventually blurred into a drone, there was a lot of white. And static. Transmitting stopped. I was an orchestra without limbs, a sky without sky. There was a re-run of an earlier scene. The same kitchen table. Same patterns in the grain of the wood. A few more scratches from where we had eaten carelessly. But otherwise the same. More tears. My mother, again making tea and toast, frowning. More talk of depression. This time, when she said I should see our doctor, I did.

35

The doctor was understanding. There had been such shame while I sat in the waiting room. I thought that everyone was staring at me, my face a banner with the phrase 'mental illness' scrawled across it in a child's handwriting. I sat opposite him in a black plastic chair. Tried to make words form sentences, struggled with a vocabulary that was then unfamiliar. He listened to me and then I listened to him and then we listened to each other. He had a lot of questions. I thought he was smart, really smart, to ask questions that were also somehow the answers. Are you sleeping too much or not at all? Do you wake early each morning or do you have trouble getting off to sleep at night? Have you lost your appetite or are you unusually hungry? Have you lost weight or gained weight? Have you lost interest in your hobbies? Is anything difficult happening in your life? I put my thoughts in his scales each time and weighed my response before answering, measuring out just the right amount of truth.

'I think it's clear,' he said, leaning forward in his chair. 'That you are suffering from severe depression.'

'It' had a name.

We had just finished talking about Elizabeth, my gap

year, whether I was taking drugs or drinking heavily, my feelings about going away to university, whether I got any exercise, whether I was thinking about suicide. When there were no more questions, he wrote out a prescription for antidepressants and warned me of likely side effects such as constipation, a dry mouth, blurred vision, drowsiness. He said that the medication wouldn't take effect for four to six weeks. It was late January. I did the sums. I wouldn't feel anything until late February at the earliest. He said that the drug he'd chosen – Prothiaden – had a sedative effect which would also medicate what he called my 'severe anxiety'. He suggested that I take up running or cycling. He also advised me to 'lay off alcohol' while I was on the antidepressants because the two wouldn't 'mix'.

I left the medical centre on legs of lead and carried my faulty brain out to the car park where a grey sun wished me dead.

36

That night, I went over to see Elizabeth. She only agreed to see me after I told her I had something really important to tell her. When she opened the front door, our old routine took charge of a tense situation. I followed her into the kitchen. She grabbed the bottle of Rémy Martin on the counter and was reaching for a tumbler when I told her I didn't want any brandy. Oh, she said, surprised. Do you want a beer instead? No. Maybe a glass of water. The taps were always too powerful. She got sprayed. We would have laughed at this a few months earlier. Now, she just swore under her breath and we sat down at the kitchen table. The TV was blaring next door. She said her mother was doing some ironing. I leaned forward and pulled her close to me. Her neck was soft and she was wearing the perfume I had bought her for Christmas. Tears came. She tried to pull me from her but I clung like a wet T-shirt.

'For god's sake,' she hissed. 'Stop crying. My mum's next door! I don't want her to see you like this.'

She shoved me hard. I let go of her.

'I saw the doctor today. He said I'm depressed. He's put me on antidepressants.'

'What?'

She sat down at the kitchen table. I wiped my eyes with my shirt sleeve. We didn't say anything for a long time. Her mother passed through the room without saying a word. I left soon after, waving to Elizabeth from my car as she stood, awkward and stunned, at the front door.

37

The next time I went over to see her, her mother answered the door and told me that Elizabeth was still in the bath. She took me into the lounge and we sat in front of the fire.

'Elizabeth told me what's going on,' she said.

'Oh right,' I said, embarrassed, thinking she was going to tell me to give up on her daughter, that she didn't love me any more.

'And I want you to know that if you ever need someone to talk to then you can count on me.'

I was surprised.

'That's very kind, thank you,' I said.

The flames cackled from across the room.

The pills were no miracle cure at first. The sedative effect wiped me out. I was drugged all day and then, just as the medication lessened its grip on me, it was time to take another pill. Then there was the furball mouth in the mornings, the constipation, the headaches, the dizziness. I went back to see my doctor after a fortnight and told him that things weren't any better. He asked me to be patient. 'I am being patient,' I said. And I was. I hadn't touched a drop of alcohol since first seeing him. It was easy then. Irritating more than anything else and, besides, I was willing to go without if it would help me get better. I dealt with the edginess of being sober by running most nights after work. I'd run until I couldn't run any more and then I'd pause somewhere out in that winter chill, bent double in the middle of nowhere and try to catch my breath. Meanwhile my parents did their best to try and pick me up. If I watched a film, my father stayed up and watched it with me. If I was alone in my bedroom at night, my mother would try to persuade me to come downstairs and watch TV. Even after three weeks, nothing seemed to be changing so my parents came up with a plan. My father was going to Boston and New York on business. They asked me if I wanted to go with him.

'The change of scenery will do you good,' they said. 'It's only for five days but you'd get to see New York.'

It was my dream to visit New York. So he took me with him. We spent nights together, going out to dinner, him trying to make sense of what was wrong with me. And then he made another dream come true by paying for us to spend the last night of the trip at the Chelsea Hotel. We had a slum of a room: the bed was full of pubic hair, there was only half a toilet seat in the bathroom and the shower curtain was covered in cigarette burns. When it was bed-time, I drifted off to sleep, happy for the first time in months, wondering if Edie Sedgwick or Patti Smith had slept in the same room.

39

Seven weeks after going on the medication, I woke up one morning and threw the bed covers back. I jumped out of bed, something I hadn't done in a long, long time. Every-thing was suddenly back to normal. It was like seeing an old friend after many years of being apart. I wanted to hug myself and say, Where have you been? I've been looking everywhere for you. It was then, only then, that I realised how sick I'd been. I opened the curtains . . .

40

No more humming. No more drone. I believed – or wanted to believe – that the medication had cured me. I had no reason not to. It was June 1989. Warm weather, blue skies. I had been to see my doctor. He took me off the antidepressants. I'd left my job at the health food store and was now working at another off-licence. I was off my chemical leash, free to roam wherever I pleased. I started drinking again as soon as the antidepressants were out of my blood. I couldn't wait. Wet throat, thirsty fangs. First moments of drunkenness warm and familiar. Glass fingers tight around the stem of my cardiac muscle. Grape tongue on hop-tipped lips. Such effortless seduction . . .

41

Elizabeth was calling again. The frequency of her calls picked up after the medication kicked in. She wanted me again, probably because 'me' had come back from a black holiday. I was new and improved. A white-toothed smile of an advertisement for antidepressants.

42

Everything was great and then my brief splash of optimism and happiness soured overnight. Getting better was a tightrope walk. It was fine until I lost my balance. I was dizzy with love as Elizabeth and I rolled in the sheets of our second honeymoon. I was back to drinking all the time. My smile slipped off my face when I wasn't looking. Sometimes there were flashes of truth and I would realise that the more I drank, the more the depression ballooned. For such a short while, I was allowed to believe that the pills had cured me forever. Now I knew, I really knew, that there was something wrong with me, something that no medicine could rectify. And so, when the depression tackled me again, I threw my hands up in the air and was slapped to the ground. The gravel was glad to see me and my split cheeks cremated into a grin.

The heat was oppressive. Mosquitoes buzzed about my face. I was taking a short cut through a thicket of bushes and trees to meet Paul and the others on time. I was drunk on a steady stream of Budweiser. I had another one on the go as I walked. I also had a razor blade in my jacket pocket. Earlier, in the bathroom at home, I had pulled it from its disposable plastic yellow shell and wrapped it in a wad of tissue. I had been obsessed for days with a passage in *The Bell Jar* where Esther Greenwood stands on a beach and says, 'I fingered the box of razors in my pocket book.' I too was dreaming of drowning myself in a loveless ocean or taking an overdose of pills or slashing my wrists.

We met outside the only local off-licence I hadn't worked at. There was a big discussion about what we were going to do – go to a pub, or a hotel bar, or the fair that had blown into town for the weekend. As the debate raged on, I unravelled the razor blade from the tissue. I crumpled the now-empty Budweiser can with my other hand. The blade came loose from the tissue. '*I fingered the box of razors in my pocket book*.' How sharp it was! I could hear everyone voting on whether or not to buy drinks from the off-licence and then head to the fair. No one was watching me. I lifted the blade from my pocket. I pressed it against the flesh of my left wrist. It was slippery in my sweaty fingers. I could hardly breathe. I pressed down and dragged the blade.

I looked down at my wrist. A red line appeared. I dragged the blade across my skin again, a little further this time. A second line appeared. Then, a third time. It was magical. The world shrank. It was like swimming underwater, there was such peace and quiet. All the pain in my head reduced to three cuts across my wrist. A million inexplicable feelings turned into a fleshy billboard. There was pain. But not a familiar pain. More like a pleasant pain. At first, it felt like someone else's pain. Borrowed. But then it was mine again.

'Are you OK?'

Paul's voice pulled me from the water. He was calling from the other side of the street. The others were busy filing into the off-licence.

'Of course,' I said, tugging my jacket sleeve over my wrist.

'Hurry up then.'

I dropped the razor blade into my pocket. Paul held the door open for me. Inside, everyone was busy choosing their drinks.

'Beer?' he said, holding up a fourpack of Grolsch.

I shook my head. I couldn't keep it a secret. I pulled my sleeve back and showed him what I couldn't seem to say.

'What the fuck have you done?' he said.

Two or three others came over. It was too late to give a shit. He pointed at my arm.

'Who has a tissue?' he said, his voice breathy with panic.

'I do,' I said.

I pulled the tissue out of my pocket and handed it to him. He snatched it and pressed it against the cuts.

'I have to get him back to my place,' he said.

They nodded. The others were laughing at the counter, oblivious, paying for their drinks.

'I didn't know it had got this bad again,' he said, as we sat at his kitchen table twenty minutes later, me sobbing uncontrollably, him digging through a dusty first-aid kit.

Nobody did.

Cutting myself became just another symptom, another language. It was like lancing a blister. That's how I knew when to stop: when the pain in my head was gone, when the skin had burst like an umbrella and shielded me from the downpour. I'd wake up from a grey sleep and realise what I was doing to myself. I'd wear long sleeves for days afterwards – even if it was a hot sunny day – and squirm if my parents or sister asked me why. Is it warm? I'd say, beads of sweat crawling down my sides. When Elizabeth and I made love, I kept my shirt on or turned the lights out. I flinched when she grabbed my wrists, her tight grip oblivious to the pain she was causing me. She would squeeze tighter and tighter until we were done and I would lie in the dark and want to scream.

45

Curls of smoke swirled off the barbecue, yawned for a moment and then flew off into the night. Paul was throwing a spontaneous party. A dozen of us were slumped on the back lawn, smoking and drinking. I was talking in hushed tones with Rebecca, a new friend of Paul's.

'Drinking is the last thing you need,' she said. 'If you're prone to depression then it's really stupid to drink every night. Which Paul says you do.'

Her green eyes locked with mine and chastised me.

'And if you get drunk,' she continued, 'then you do things like slash your wrists when you're out with friends.'

She raised her eyebrows. They were brown. Her hair was dyed red, a deep, dark red.

'Oh Paul told you about that.'

Paul was useless at keeping secrets. He had already told me that Rebecca was manic depressive and taking lithium. He had given me the whole story – suicide attempts, spells in hospital, diagnosis, lithium, therapy – after smoking some mind-blowing pot.

'Listen,' she said, as she nibbled on a smile-shaped slice of raw onion. 'The only thing that numbs depression is death. Think about it.'

She ate the rest of the onion. She was so pale. Her skin had a yellowish hue to it. Paul said this was because of the lithium.

'I know,' I said, feeling sheepish because I had a beer in my hand.

'This is my last try,' she said, tucking a strand of that red hair behind her ear. 'If you're prone to depression and you drink, then you're doubling the depression because alcohol is a depressant. Follow me? Right. Now think of a bird taking a plane ride from A to B. Why pay for a set of wings when you've already got a perfectly good pair?'

46

My grandfather died at the end of August. My reaction to his death was muted. I think I was suspended in a state of disbelief. My grief was packed in ice and dropped far into my subconscious. When the funeral service ended, the blood-red curtain to the right of the coffin whirred into action. It was drawn on runners until it covered the coffin, bit by bit, little by little. And then he was gone. I had never been to a funeral before and later that night, lying in bed, my mind short-circuited on the images of the day: the way the sunlight streamed through the windows and struck the coffin, the messages on the cards, the cufflinks my grandmother thrust into my hand, the long journey home, the way the cold beer I drank that night reacted with a sensitive tooth I had at the time.

47

Dawn was crawling up on the world. The sun was already bright. Elizabeth had left her shoes on the beach and was paddling in the sea. Waves were caressing her ankles. She was wearing all white. There wasn't a cloud in the sky. We were in Corfu. Our holiday was almost over. A hangover was rising in my skull. My eyes angry slits. I couldn't think of anything to say. We were all talked out. Drunk and exhausted, we had wandered in silence along the beach, she ten or so paces ahead of me, me following her footsteps in the sand.

48

Tower blocks. The sludge of Deptford Creek. Yellow lights. Barges and cargo boats. A traffic jam all the way down to Greenwich. A hall of residence: eight-foot-high walls, barbed wire, facing a cemetery. A short walk to the spot where Christopher Marlowe got stabbed in the eye. My room overlooked a concrete courtyard. I arrived with

two cases of beer and pockets filled with packs of cigarettes. No sooner had my father closed the door on my new
room than I sat down on the bed, lit a cigarette and
cracked open a can of beer.

49

I took two cans of Miller Lite down to the first hall dinner.
The other students had beakers of fruit juice or glasses of
water or cups of coffee or mugs of tea. When I cracked the
first ring-pull – it was just after six – everyone stared.

50

If we didn't want to be disturbed in the morning by the
cleaners, we had to put our wastepaper bin outside our door
at bed-time. I turned up to the first few breakfasts hung over
and then stopped going. I started to put my bin outside my
door. Typically, it was full of crumpled beer cans, deflated
cartons of orange juice, empty bottles of vodka and heaps of
cigarette ash, topped off with countless cigarette butts. It
took no more than a fortnight for the gossiping to start. One
morning, I woke up to voices outside my door.

'Shit,' said a voice I didn't recognise. 'Look at his bin.'

'I know,' said someone else. 'It's like that every morning.'

'Is he an alcoholic?' I heard another girl say.

'Looks like it,' said a male voice. I recognised the voice.
It was the student hall monitor. 'Every morning, his bin's
overflowing. It's getting scary.'

'What are you going to do about it?' said the first girl.

'Tell Meadows,' said the hall monitor.

I pulled the covers over my head. Meadows – a frantic, sweaty man with a passion for Elizabethan literature and heavy drinking – was the hall director. He was also one of my course tutors.

51

Three drunken students taped objects to the ceiling of my tiny room: books, cassettes, slices of bread, cutlery and even an open umbrella, tied to the light fitting. One student abandoned his giant home-made bong long enough to vanish and return with an opened can of rice pudding which he poured into the umbrella. I spent most of the party shotgunning cans of Budweiser while The Replacements blasted from my stereo. Sometime, deep in the night, Meadows stormed into the room and shouted at me. I got a written warning the following morning. I sat reading it beneath the rice-pudding-filled umbrella. I was charged with 'Excessive noise disturbance'. I threw the letter down into a pool of stale beer.

52

I often drank a can of beer before going to classes, even the ones that started at 9.30 am. I remember the fitness freak student who lived in the room opposite me shaking his head when he saw me sipping a beer in the corridor at 8.45 one morning.

'Don't you ever stop?' he said.

I crumpled the can in my hand.

'Evidently not.'

53

'Where are you going?'

I was pulling my jeans on. It was almost 5am.

'Back to my room.'

I didn't really know whose room I was in. I knew her name was Caroline and I knew that she was studying psychology but that was about it.

'Guilty about cheating on your girlfriend?'

'Something like that.'

A student on my floor called Andy had thrown a party. Caroline and I talked all night, our tongues loosened by Andy's lethal joints and bottles of budget-priced vinegary wine. When she was trashed her brown eyes took on a dirty glaze and smoke rings cuffed our wrists together until time passed and we were in her bed, our limbs tangled like threads of wet tobacco. And then, hours later, when the pot and wine had worn off, we were two strangers hiding in the dark.

'I've got a boyfriend. You're not the only one who feels bad here.'

I was crouched down, lacing my shoes up.

'I know.'

What had I done? I was confused. I thought of Elizabeth. And then I looked at the naked woman looking at me.

'Go on then,' she said. 'Get out of here.'

I went back to my room.

I opened a can of beer, lay on my bed and stared at the ceiling.

Elizabeth and I talked on the phone most nights but there was little to say. She was still at school, I was away at university. She was living with her parents, I was living alone. Our phone calls crackled with awkward silences. Were we drifting apart? Was it over? Would I tell her about this? I was due to meet Elizabeth later that morning in Kensington. What had I done to her? I got up. I was unsteady on my feet, drunker than I thought. I grabbed a disposable razor from under the sink. I shattered the plastic shell with the heel of a shoe. I pulled the blade free. I sat back down on the lip of my bed . . .

When she took me in her arms at the station, nasty cuts snarled beneath my shirt sleeves. Just like old times. We went for coffee. I couldn't tell her. She seemed so kind, so loving. She made me feel dirty and soiled. When it was time for her to leave, I flinched when she said she loved me because only hours before I had been with someone else, someone who had somehow replaced her, someone I had wanted like I hadn't wanted Elizabeth in a long time.

I called her the following evening and – with a bottle of vodka inside me – broke up with her.

'But why,' she kept saying, crying.

'Because we've grown apart,' I repeated over and over. 'Because we've grown apart.'

When I went home for Reading Week in November 1989, I saw the doctor again. I was pasty-faced, gaunt. Couldn't sleep. So much cutting, drinking, smoking. The doctor listened again. I gave him the inventory of my recent life: my grandfather's death, the break-up with Elizabeth, moving out of home. I edited out the best bits: the bits that I thought would get me committed. The sad comfort of a razor blade, the slap of a breakfast beer, the days when I didn't wake up until late afternoon. He said I had lost 'an alarming amount of weight', and for a second time diagnosed me as suffering from severe depression and anxiety.

He wrote out a prescription for the same antidepressant as before, reminding me that the sedative effect would help control the anxiety. He warned me again that I shouldn't drink alcohol while taking the medication. This time, though, I didn't give a fuck. I had no intention of quitting drinking. That was all I had left. I really believed this. He asked me to see my university doctor as soon as I went back because she needed to monitor my progress.

Later that night, I stood in the kitchen, with a little red pill in the palm of my hand and thought, Here we go again. The dry mouth, the drowsiness, the check-ups, the constipation, the foggy brain . . . the medicated merry-go-round, the short-term relief . . . and then what?

55

The university doctor was impatient and curt with me.

'Are you contemplating suicide?' she asked.

I stared at her. Contemplating? That made it sound so rational, like do I want toast or cereal for breakfast . . .

'No,' I said, telling myself that I was in for a sprained ankle.

She was icy, disinterested.

'Are you happy with the dose you're on?'

How could I be happy being on antidepressants?

'It isn't working,' I said. 'If that's what you're asking.'

'Let's raise the dose then.'

She scribbled out a prescription that would make it almost impossible for me to wake up before one or two in the afternoon.

56

During the next fortnight, I dyed my hair orange, then dark brown and finally black. I got my ear pierced. I skipped most of my classes. I smoked forty, fifty cigarettes a day. I cut myself. I drank from the moment I was awake until the moment I wasn't. Got stoned all the time. Barely ate anything. I lost so much weight that my clothes hung off me. I had dark circles under my eyes. I missed Elizabeth. I missed my parents. I missed my grandfather. I went back to the doctor and told her the pills still weren't working. She referred me to a psychiatrist.

57

The psychiatrist had silver hair and red puffy hamster cheeks. He greeted my attempts to tell him how desperate I felt with a glassy stare and a rapidly scrawled prescription for what he called a 'booster drug'. I don't know what he gave me but he said it would work in combination with the antidepressants I was already taking. My appointment was over in less than ten minutes. We talked – rather, I talked – about the medication I was taking. He asked me how I was 'getting on with it' and then he leafed through a big, fat medicine book and picked out this 'booster drug' like he was a tired magician who had pulled the rabbit out of the hat one too many times.

58

Kristen was an American student on an exchange programme. She wore only black and loved The Cure. She was snow-pale and never drank alcohol. When I asked her why – as if there was something wrong with her because she didn't drink – she said she didn't like feeling out of control. We were introduced by another American student in my hall and within minutes she was mothering me. The friendship that ensued was brief and intense. By the time we were getting to know each other, she was on her way back to California. But years later, she would play an enormous part in changing my life. Whenever I saw her, she took to dragging me back to her hall where she would feed me pasta. 'You have to eat,' she would say as she chopped tomatoes and garlic. 'Look at you. You're so thin.' She was the only friend at university who seemed to care when I told her that I was going to start seeing a psychiatrist. 'I think this will help,' she said. 'You really need to talk to someone.' The night after my first appointment, I drank thirteen pints of beer and then took my new spread of pills. I woke up the next morning on a friend's floor. On the way back to my own hall, my left arm and leg suddenly turned numb. The paralysis only lasted a few seconds but it was scary enough to make me call Kristen from a pay phone. She listened to what I was telling her and then she fell silent. 'You can't drink on top of all that medication,' she warned. 'You're going to get sick.' She invited me over for dinner that night. I tried to get out of it but she insisted. I hung up and went back to my room and slept until it was dark again. When we were in the kitchen, her making her killer pasta, me sipping a glass of sugary red wine, she turned to me, the scent of fresh basil all over her fingers and said, 'Just tell me why you're drinking with your medication even though you know how stupid it is and I'll shut up.' She was too close. I was frightened. 'I love the smell of fresh basil,' I said. 'Makes me dream of the time I went on holiday to Italy with my family.' She went back to chopping the herb. Chop. Chop. Chop. Blows heavy enough to mark the cutting board.

59

I saw the psychiatrist once a fortnight. Every appointment was a replay of the first. As I walked from my room to the medical centre, I rehearsed speeches that I never got to say. Each meeting was short and procedural. In early December, at our last appointment before the end of term, I turned up with cuts on my left wrist. When we sat down, he began – as always – by asking me how I was doing. I rolled up my shirt sleeve and said, 'This is how I'm doing.

There's no other way to explain it.' He opened his book of medicines and said, 'I see.' Minutes later, he wrote out another prescription, putting me on an even higher dose.

60

On Christmas day, I stood at the lounge window and looked for my grandfather when the car pulled into the driveway. My grandmother was in the passenger seat and her daughter, my aunt, was driving. For a second, a dirty pane of glass between us, I hoped that it might all have been a bad dream and that he would be in the back seat, grey hair swept back, distinguished, wearing his favourite beige cardigan. I took a sip of champagne. The car doors swung open. My father went outside to help his mother out of the car. When we were all pulling crackers, eating Christmas lunch, his absence sat at the table like it was a new member of the family.

61

When I went back to university, I hadn't had a drink for five days. I'd been to see my doctor at home for a repeat prescription. When he found out that I was still drinking, he ordered me to stop immediately because the alcohol would be counteracting the effects of the antidepressants. Once term began, I caught up on course work and wrote overdue papers. Insomnia plagued me. I locked myself in at night, hiding from the knuckles that rapped on the door. I wrote poems and short stories, read Raymond

Carver, chain-smoked. In the early hours of the morning, drunken screams bounced off the hall's courtyard. My will was weak. I can't tell you when or why I started drinking again. I can only tell you that I did.

62

Andy dropped acid. I didn't want to so I bought six cans of Carlsberg Special Brew and got drunk instead. When I finished the final can, he was peaking and looked so happy. I wanted a piece of that happiness. So I took a tab. He was the drug king in our hall. He was supplying everyone with pot, speed, mushrooms, acid. We were listening to The Butthole Surfers in his room. Everything was great, euphoric, amazing and then all of a sudden, I wanted to be alone. I went to my room. I remember locking the door but then everything goes black. The next thing I knew, Andy was standing over me. I had torn posters off my wall, trashed heaps of cassettes, thrown clothes everywhere. I had also cut my left arm. Deep, dangerous cuts that would leave scars forever. Andy said he had been pounding on my door for twenty minutes. I remembered nothing other than waking up and unlocking the door and him bursting in. And then I saw the wreckage. And I had no idea how it happened. He went and got a student from next door – Mike, from my course – and the two of them cleaned the wounds and pressed Kleenex on my arm until the bleeding stopped. 'Thank fuck for that,' Andy said as he eased plasters on to my arm. 'I couldn't have taken you to hospital in the state you're in. And besides, I'm tripping my brains out.'

After two more written warnings from Meadows for throwing loud parties, he slipped a note under my door asking me to see him. I should throw you out of the hall for being a nuisance, he said. But I know you've been having some problems. I told him about the ongoing depression, the antidepressants, the psychiatrist. He said he already knew all about this. Everyone in the English department is worried about the amount you drink, he said. I think you're an alcoholic, Nick. You need help. He asked me to come clean about my drinking at my next appointment with the psychiatrist. I want you to report back after you've seen him. I'm not letting you off the hook. I understand, I said, and left his office.

64

The psychiatrist leafed through his book of medicines. I had come to hate that book because he was more interested in it than me. I had just told him the Meadows story but had been careful not to use the word 'alcoholic'. He was as steely as ever. No reaction. No raised eyebrows. Just the sound of that big, fat book being slapped on his thighs. He flicked through it, his brow infuriatingly attentive. I just wanted him to tell me why I was doing what I was doing.

'I'm going to prescribe you another type of medication,' he said. 'It's called Antabuse. It's a drug to stop patients from drinking.'

Stop patients from drinking?

'What is it?' I asked.

He looked up from his prescription pad.

'It's a drug which first came into use in the treatment of alcoholics in the nineteen fifties. Once it's in your system, it makes you violently sick if you drink while taking it. If you mix alcohol with it then you'll be physically ill in a way that you've never experienced. Under no circumstances can you mix the two. Is that clear?'

'Yes,' I said. 'Very clear.'

No alcohol. I walked home with the Antabuse tablets in a chemist's bag. I toyed with the idea of throwing the bag in a bin and pretending to take it. I knew I needed it though. *The treatment of alcoholics.* Back in my room, I smoked a cigarette and stared out the window. Nineteen and being prescribed Antabuse. I popped the first of the Antabuse pills on to my tongue and tried to think of a way of not having to swallow it but there wasn't one. I went down to dinner. I had never noticed before how bland the food was and how dirty the trays were.

65

A week after I went home for Easter break I decided to flush every last Antabuse tablet down the toilet. I couldn't stand being sober. After working out from the leaflet in the packet that it would take five days to clean the drug out of my bloodstream, I figured that five days was the perfect amount of time to get all the reading I needed to get done out the way. That way I'd clean-sweep the exams and hang on to my place on the course. It was an ingenious plan, and by the time the exams were over in May, I had not only passed every single one of them but I was free to drink as much as I liked. I stopped turning up to my appointments with the psychiatrist and I avoided Meadows at all costs. I knelt down by the rivers of alcohol and drank deeply, laughed, tried to drown myself.

66

The early-morning traffic was buzzing outside. Laura got out of bed, rested her elbows on the window sill and smoked a cigarette. She was studying English and French, so some of our classes overlapped. Somehow, our brains pickled with cheap red wine, we had ended up in bed together. I'd been out drinking with Mike who'd become a good friend after playing nurse during that disastrous acid trip. I was avoiding Andy at all costs and instead spending nights with Mike talking about our mutual fascination with Marlon Brando and Mickey Rourke. On that particular night, he and I ran into Laura and her best friend Chloe by the hall cigarette machine. We ended up going to Chloe's room. She opened several bottles of red wine, and when they were empty, Laura and I went off to her room . . .

'Are you feeling guilty?' I asked, knowing she had a serious boyfriend.

'Guilty about what?'

Her body tensed up, her shoulder blades reaching towards one another like hesitant lovers, poised to kiss for the first time.

'Your boyfriend.'

She blew a cool line of smoke out of her mouth.

'This is a mistake,' she said.

There was a long silence and then she put her cigarette out and came back to bed.

'So you know I'm seeing someone?'

'The ski instructor. He lives in Austria doesn't he?'

'How do you know?'

'Everyone knows everything in this place.'

And they did. Earlier that night, I had pretended that I needed to go to my room to get another pack of cigarettes. She insisted on tagging along with me. I turned my back to her and took my antidepressants. I was sure that if she knew I was on medication, she would run a mile. Months later, when I asked her why she hadn't wanted to know what the pills were, she laughed and said that everyone in the hall knew that I was on them.

67

My initial impression of Laura – based on hall gossip, casual encounters, sharing those occasional classes – was that she was the kind of girl who'd not only let you destroy yourself but would probably come along for the ride. Everyone said she was a big pot-head. She always looked stoned, floating around in her black leather jacket and hippie beads. She had mischievous eyes. A slight sneer. A sarcastic sense of humour. She had a jaded air about her too that suggested a dulled nostalgia for better days.

Once we were spending time together – and there was no reference to any kind of 'relationship' – she turned out to be shy and introverted. She'd grown up in a rural part of Berkshire and found living in London daunting. The rumours were right – she was stoned all the time – but it was a coping mechanism, a way to take the edge off all the changes going on in her life. She also drank a lot to overcome her shyness and under-confidence. And then, when she was drunk and stoned, she was transformed into her sexually aggressive, wild, adventurous, thrill-seeking alter ego, and it was this chemical doppelgänger that I fell in love with. Not the real her.

We spent the last few weeks of term staying up all night, drinking, laughing, fooling around in bed. We had a lot of fun. Sometimes we woke up in the middle of the afternoon, nursing gigantic hangovers and she'd chuckle as I fixed us Alka Seltzer in dirty glasses that we had used the night before to shoot tequila. We would smoke a few cigarettes, drink some foul tasting instant coffee and then make love, the previous night's alcohol oozing from our pores as we clung to one another like sinking ships, her sweaty little moans like flares going off against the stunned silence of my retreating depression. Everything was fine, more than fine, as long as we didn't mention her 'other boyfriend'.

Laura and this phantom boyfriend had been together since they were sixteen. She said he was her 'first love'. But when I asked too many questions – like why is her first love in Austria and not with her – she'd get testy and change the subject. She hated anyone getting too close to her. Inside, she was a vacuum, a black hole, and her biggest fear was that one day someone would find out. She used sarcasm as a shield and she had a sharp, mean tongue on her. She hid behind her cleverness and used it to manipulate everyone around her. I was always trying to get closer to her but the more I pushed, the more she pulled back.

68

Summer rolled before me, as endless as the fields that framed Laura's parents' house. I went to stay there as often as I could. We were both busy with holiday jobs. She worked as a waitress and I temped, loading trucks and working in warehouses. July and August flew by as we spent weekends getting drunk on Portuguese rosé. In the early hours of the morning – when her parents were fast asleep next door – we would roll drunkenly around on her bedroom floor, trying to have the quietest sex possible. When I was back at my parents' house, I missed her all the time. We rang each other every night, sharing the details of our mundane lives. Afterwards, I spent empty nights getting drunk at local pubs with the old gang.

69

On the surface, it seemed that she wasn't really interested in helping me to get better but then, little things happened that surprised me. One night, in the middle of dinner with her parents, her mother handed me a folded piece of note paper.

'What's this?' I asked, taking it from her.

'It's a number for Depression Fellowship.'

I didn't know she knew. I cringed and turned bright red

as if she'd said something like: *So you and my daughter are sleeping together.*

'I read about it in a paper,' she explained. 'You can call them and they'll help you, any time, day or night.'

'Thank you,' I said.

When I asked Laura, after dinner, if she and her mother had been talking about me, she shrugged and said that, yes, she was worried about me, and yes, her mother wanted to help me. But I never called the fellowship. I was too scared that they'd lock me up, too frightened of what might happen if I told the truth.

70

One weekend, when her parents were away, Laura bought some speed from a Hell's Angel. She cut two white lines on the kitchen table. The high was bright and electric, pricked with tiny epiphanies where just for a moment, a precious moment, the world was revolving around us rather than us around it. The remarkable zest of our trajectory blinded time. We were pathetic children, pretty paper planes in tropical rain. We stayed up all night, playing records, drinking warm beer, laughing, eventually rushing upstairs to bed. After we made love, my mood crashed and folded against cruel tarmac, flames calmly taking flesh from bone with the finesse of a loving butcher. I told her all about my grandfather's funeral in minute detail. She said very little, lying beside me, listening. When I finished the story, the room was quiet. She was asleep. I had been talking to myself. I wondered if I heard what I was trying to say.

Laura came out of the shower. Her hair was soaking wet, she wrapped a towel around herself.

'Are you serious?'

I had just told her that I wanted to throw my anti-depressants down the toilet.

'Yes,' I said. 'I want to do it. I'm sick of these things. It's no life to keep popping pills.'

She frowned.

'Shouldn't you see a doctor first?'

I wanted to tell her how much I loved her, that it was her who had made me feel alive again, but I couldn't. She refused to clarify if she had broken things off with her old boyfriend yet. She also made a point of telling me that she didn't want to get into what she called the 'I love you stuff'. She said it was fake and she wanted to 'keep things fun'. In spite of this, I believed I was happier than I had been in a long while because I wasn't cutting. It wasn't that the urge had gone – it hadn't, it was there, strong as ever, seductive as ever: how I craved the simplicity of shrinking my problems into the sweep of a razor blade across my skin – it was just that I was terrified of what she would do if she knew. Just like I was terrified of what my parents would do if they knew.

'Why? How can they tell if I'm happy? Besides, I stopped seeing that asshole psychiatrist months ago.'

She shook her head. A fine spray flew from her hair.

'Do whatever you think is best,' she said.

I went into the bathroom and flushed them goodbye.

'Laura? I'm telling you I love you, doesn't that mean anything?'

It was September 1990. Mike and I had moved into an old place in Deptford. She wouldn't move into a house with Chloe until a few days before our second year started.

'You know I do,' she said through clenched teeth.

All summer, the lack of definition had been eating away at me. I didn't want to share her. I wanted her all to myself.

'How am I supposed to know if you don't tell me?'

'You just should.'

'I need to hear you say it.'

'This is getting boring, I have to go.'

'Why?'

'I'm going out in a minute.'

'So that's it?'

'Bye Nick. I've got to run.'

She hung up on me. I went to the refrigerator, pulled out the chilled litre of white wine that I was saving for another night, plopped myself down in one of the big old armchairs and drank.

Once term began, Laura and I argued all the time about her refusal to commit to our relationship. The more intense I got, the more she ran from me. I'd be out drinking with Mike and see her flirting with other men at the campus bar. If I asked her what she was doing, she'd laugh and tell me that I was 'too possessive'. Mike kept telling me that Laura was too immature for a serious relationship, that she was so insecure that she needed two boyfriends to make herself feel whole. And this was how that winter played out. There were arguments and tears and vodka and drugs. We were only happy when we were in bed and then – with life shut out – everything was perfect. There were long nights spent making love, our bodies numbed with alcohol and pot. She played games all the time: saying she'd call and then not call, saying she had broken up with the other boyfriend only for me to then lie in her bed and listen to her talk with him on the phone next door in a hushed voice. Whenever I asked her why he had rung or why there was a letter lying on the dresser from him, she would sigh and ignore me. I was always getting sick. I got bronchitis three times that winter. She wore me down. The first time I got it, the college doctor asked me what had happened to the anti-depressants. I told her that I had been feeling better and stopped taking them. She said I should have asked her about it first. Too late, I thought, as she wrote out a new prescription, for another dose of antibiotics.

74

We were at the campus bar. It was Tequila Night. Shots for 50p. Laura and I got so drunk that we couldn't stop laughing. Tears streaming down our faces, cheekbones aching from the inside out. Suddenly, she threw her arms around me and told me she loved me. It was the first time she had said it. She took my hand and led me down to the toilets. After checking that no one was in the female toilets, she rushed me into a cubicle and bolted the door behind us. She unzipped my trousers and then pushed me down on to the toilet seat. She lifted her skirt, peeled her panties down, pulled them over her ankles and boots and stuffed them in her jacket pocket. She straddled me and made love to me like she needed me, wanted me, loved me. When we finished, she clung to me and for a blissful minute, I truly believed she loved me and only me.

75

Mike dared me to shoot a glass of vodka through my nose. He said he had heard that it got you really drunk. I lay back on the carpet. He handed me a glass. I raised my head and pinched my right nostril shut. I held the shot glass to my left nostril and tipped it back. I saw stars. Carnivals. Ferris wheels. Bright lights. Candy-floss. My funeral. Granite stone. The rest of the night, we drank vodka shots the regular way. Later, I threw up all over myself, down my front, in my lap, all over the carpet.

76

This latest 'honeymoon' was over in a matter of days. As soon as she was better, Laura went back to her old ways: the letters and hushed phone calls, the games. It got so we couldn't be in the same room. We were like two fighting cats. Our love became a scab that neither of us could stop picking at. One day I was too tired to pick any more. And then, when I was exhausted, the depression rolled over me like it always did.

There were days when I didn't get out of bed until it was dark. On others I didn't go to bed at all. I rarely went to classes. The kitchen sink was stacked high with dirty dishes. I was too tired to run a bath, shave, wash my hair. Mike – keen to avoid the stench of my decay – spent increasing amounts of time at his brother's house. I wore the same clothes day in, day out. I couldn't see any point in changing them. Sometimes my eyes would open and I'd find myself fully clothed, a can of beer by my bed. I rang people all the time. I called my mother every day to talk about my latest argument with Laura. I often called Dennis in the early hours of the morning, waking him up to tell him I was thinking of killing myself. I never remembered making these calls until Dennis rang the next day to see if I was still alive. He would tell me what I had said and I would feel ashamed. I'm sorry, I'd say, another mantra that now coursed through my everyday life. I'm sorry.

The cutting was back too. Laura got hysterical when she saw cuts for the first time. She said I was 'sick' and called me 'a freak'. No matter how hard I tried to explain that it helped me, that it made things easier, more tolerable, the look of disgust and revulsion on her face wouldn't shift. Another night, she called by to find I'd cut again and it was too much for her.

'Why don't you just kill yourself and get it over with?'

she shouted. 'If you're really serious then I'll go and get a razor blade and you can slash your fucking wrists and it'll all be over. Do you want me to go and get a razor blade? Do you? Because I can't take this any more.'

Laura didn't understand. I stared at her through a blizzard of tears. We'd been going out for six months and still she didn't get 'it', just like nobody got 'it'. I didn't want to die. That was my biggest fear, the last thing I wanted to happen. I wanted to kill the depression though. I wanted to murder it. To bleed it out of my body.

'Is that a no?' she shouted. 'Is it?'

I nodded.

'What's wrong with you?' I said.

'What's wrong with me? How can you ask that? You're the fucked-up mess, not me. I'm going to call your parents in the morning and tell them that you're out of control.'

'Don't you dare.'

'Why not?'

Long pause.

'Because it would kill them if they knew about this.'

She stubbed her cigarette out and poured herself another shot of vodka. I took the bottle out of her hand and swigged from it. We didn't say anything for ten, maybe fifteen minutes. Then, in stony silence, when the vodka ran out, we made love on the floor, half-dressed. Afterwards, she crawled into bed. I lit a cigarette and went in search of a half-drunk, stale can of beer that I remembered seeing on the kitchen window sill earlier in the evening.

Alcohol's winter lullabies sang me into a black trance. Laura's love was a slap in the face. My face was a sheet of white paper with two eyes, a nose and a mouth drawn on it. The house was empty. The orange plastic rectangular casing called me to the bathroom. I took it in my hands. I put it under my shoe. The razor blade slipped free. It was like watching Laura pull her dress over her head. The nakedness astonished me. I dragged the blade across the inside of my arm, once, twice, three times and then the music carried me away. Endorphins rushed like champagne bubbles to the scene of the crime. There was a commotion in my body. I was far away, on a mental holiday, walking sandy beaches, the sun burning my skin. When I came back, there was pain. Not a bad kind of pain. But an understanding pain. A physical pain that was better than the sick drone of my depressive brain spiralling into coffins of twisted logic. I poured another gigantic glass of vodka. I sipped at it, blood streaking my skin like a blind painter's brush-strokes, the deafening thunderstorm of my thoughts reduced to the drip-drip of post-cutting relief.

'Is going insane a real fear for you?'

My doctor was eyeing me with concern. I'd seen her so many times by this point that it felt like she was no longer sure what to do with me.

'I guess so.'

I had told her that I thought I was going insane. This

seemed – to me – to be an accurate description of what was going on in my brain.

She tapped her pen on her knee.

'I don't know what to suggest,' she said. 'I can put you back on antidepressants or I can refer you to the medical centre's counselling team. What do you want to do?'

I didn't want any more pills. I was sick of them.

'I think I need to talk to someone.'

'Let's try counselling then. The first step is for you to make an appointment to see one of the counsellors for a psychiatric evaluation. Then, based on what the counsellor decides, we'll take it from there. OK? Go back to the reception and make an appointment.' The receptionist said that it was going to be ten days before I could see a counsellor.

Ten days . . .

81

A woman in her mid-thirties called out my name. I followed her upstairs to her office. She reminded me of an actress. I couldn't think which one at first and then it came to me: she looked a bit like Debra Winger.

'My name is Veronica,' she said, sitting down in a black leather armchair. 'I'm going to do the psychiatric evaluation.'

A tall, healthy tree stood behind, outside, beyond the window. During our weekly sessions, which would last for the next eighteen months, this tree watched me shiver and sweat through the different seasons. I sat down in another leather armchair opposite her. There was a table to my left, with a box of tissues and a spider plant on it.

'First, I have to tell you that if you appear to be in danger of harming yourself or others, I have to inform your doctor.'

I knew that I would – under no circumstances – mention the cutting.

'I understand.'

The walls closed in on me. I was scared.

'It's also important', she added, 'that you're as honest as you can be at all times.'

'I'll do my best,' I said.

Veronica asked me a lot of questions and made notes as I answered them. She wanted to know what symptoms I was experiencing and ran through a check-list (I answered yes to all of them); how much I drank (as much as my friends: the usual lie), how much I smoked (forty a day), did I take drugs? (no: another lie), why had I not wanted antidepressants? (they don't work: a delusion), had I seen a counsellor before? (no), was I in a relationship? (yes), what was that like? (dysfunctional, destructive, mutually abusive: not that I knew this then), what was my relationship with my family like? (good but I was keeping a lot of secrets from them), was I having problems with my course work? (just getting by), how and when I had been depressed before? (a long story), was I suicidal? (no: maybe).

I watered every answer down, making sure the response stayed within my perception of what constituted 'normal' and what constituted 'get locked up'.

'I think you are suffering from a combination of severe depression and anxiety,' she concluded, her diagnosis rhyming beautifully with the ones that came before. 'I recommend that you start seeing a counsellor here on a weekly basis who can work through some of your problems with you and try to get to the bottom of why you keep getting depressed.'

'OK.'

I had a lump in my throat. It felt right. No more pills. But instead this . . .

'Would you like to see me or another female counsellor or a male counsellor?'

'I would like to see you,' I said.

She smiled. It was an 'I get you' smile. Hope spilled from her mouth.

82

What happened over the next eighteen months between me and Veronica in that little room remains sacred, almost holy in my memory. It was step one of many. It was a start. It was the beginning of me turning my life around. She taught me how to analyse my moods, how to examine insurmountable feelings from a different perspective, how to decipher emotions that I wanted to run from, how to identify behavioural patterns, how to understand why I did what I did, how to see my life as a grid of repetitions and motifs, how our relationships with others are reflections of our inner selves, how we develop coping systems and mechanisms that are dangerous and unhealthy. Our work together was slow. Often painfully so. She was always fighting my self-destructiveness, my tendency to shut down, to close off, to become unreachable. She'd push me and I would resent her. I'd run from her and she'd resent me. Sometimes I'd show up hung over and sick just to spite her. Sometimes I'd be eager to please and would enthusiastically respond to visualisation techniques and other such forms that she used to try and get inside my heart. And then there were sessions when she would just get plain angry with me.

'Trying to run away from your problems isn't the answer. The amount you're drinking is not only damaging your health, it's also clouding over any hope of you resolving your problems. Until you step out from this mask, things are going to stay foggy.'

Veronica sat back in her chair, never breaking direct eye contact. I'd been seeing her for two months. There was a deliberate pause and then she said it.

'I think you're an alcoholic.'

I looked away. We sat there in silence, me red and flustered, staring out at the tree, until the session came to an end.

83

Laura and I split up just before term ended. She said we needed to take a 'holiday' from each other and, rather than fight any more, I agreed. Once the Easter break started, I knew I wouldn't see Veronica for a month. On the first night, I was alone. Mike had gone to his parents' house to get some revision done. I knew I'd hit a dead end. Either I stopped killing myself with drink and nailed down to some exam revision or I kept drinking. I took the sensible option, drank four cans of beer and went to bed at 9pm. I woke up at 8am feeling refreshed, having slept right through the night. As if fate had been working while I was asleep, a packet from my mother arrived in the post. It was a Rescue Remedy tincture for depression. I put some in a glass of water as instructed and hoped for the best. Then I set about trying to sort the flat out. I cleaned the dishes. I washed my clothes. I laid bait for the mice that ran freely. I bought food and then I went about catching up on course work with military precision. I set myself the following goal: go out and buy a bottle of Piat d'Or red wine every morning after breakfast. Then, work for twelve hours. Once the work was done, I allowed myself the bottle of wine. It was alcoholic logic: put a drink on the end of the task and it's amazing how fast the task gets done. After clearing most of the backlog, I felt better, more stable. And by drinking only a single bottle of wine a night, my spirits lifted. Everything was looking up . . .

84

Veronica wasn't impressed. I sat opposite her, a colossal hangover making me sweat and cough.

'Why would you take Laura back? She said that she was with her old boyfriend for the whole of Easter. Why can't you leave it alone?'

Once I had taken and passed all of my exams – thanks to my alcohol-as-reward system working its magic – I spent a lot of time with Laura. We got along well for a fortnight, drinking, making love, having fun . . . it was like the old days. Honeymoon number 103.

'I thought things would be different this time.'

I hadn't seen her at all over Easter. I thought we were finished. She dropped by the night before the exams started. She said that the ski instructor had been back for the whole of Easter: a month. I told her I'd slept with someone else. It evened things out – now she was jealous too. When she left that night, she kissed me. It was hopeless. We couldn't keep our hands off each other.

'And was it different this time?'

The harmony vanished as it always did and then we were fighting again about the same tired things: her on/off ex-boyfriend, the games she played, my drinking.

'For a week or two.'

Veronica sighed.

'Why can't you see she's bad for you?'

'Because I love her.'

I broke into another coughing fit.

'Drinking and smoking damage the immune system. Are you aware that you're destroying your health?'

I couldn't answer her because I was coughing so hard.

'You're wrecking your body.'

'I know.'

The problem was, by this point, getting drunk was as natural for me as cleaning my teeth. It was just something I did.

85

It came from nowhere. Whoosh. A sudden wash of bile. Mike and I had been out drinking. I ran to the bathroom, fighting to keep it down. And then I vomited. A jet, a wave, a hurricane. There hadn't been any time to turn the lights on. My nostrils stung from the ferocity of the vomiting. I retched several times. I groped around in the dark for the toilet paper, tore off a handful and wiped my mouth. Then I backed up and flicked the light switch on. Stars flickered before my eyes. I caught my reflection in the bathroom mirror – chalky pale, clammy, charcoal-grey half-moon beneath each eye. I moved to flush the toilet. Before my hand reached the handle . . . I saw a glimpse of something red. I leaned closer, unsteady on my feet, to see better. Strings of blood, blobs of blood, specks of blood. I tried to think of something red that I had eaten or drunk so that I could blame what I was seeing on a tomato or red wine but I had been drinking vodka-grapefruit all night and I only ate a toasted cheese sandwich all day. I flushed, killed the light and went to bed.

86

It was a Saturday night. Laura and I had split up again. I was home alone, guzzling wine in front of a depressing episode of *Thirtysomething*. A plot thread in the show – maybe Nancy having cancer, Gary dying, I don't remember what – upset me. I went to the bathroom and got a razor blade. I made several cuts on my arms. Drops of blood fell on to my grubby white T-shirt, bloomed like red roses and wilted into dark red stains.

87

On the last night of term, I saw Laura across a crowded bar. I blanked her. She blanked me. I was drinking and flirting with a girl from my course called Claudia. I asked Claudia if she wanted to go back to my flat and split a bottle of wine. Why not? she said. I took her face in my hands and kissed her. We walked back to my place, drank the wine and went to bed. In the morning, after she got dressed and left for summer break, I made some coffee and, for the first time in ages, knew that Veronica was right, there was life after Laura.

88

I spent four weeks that summer travelling around the States on a Greyhound bus. It was a gift from my parents for my twenty-first birthday. It was also an attempt to shock me back to life. When my father had taken me to New York before it had worked. They were desperate to 'fix' me and this was their latest plan. I remember I got a lump in my throat when they suggested it because they were trying so hard and I didn't know how to tell them that there was nothing they could do to help me.

I got on a bus in New York – after spending a week on a friend's sofa – and travelled straight down the East Coast. I arrived in Athens, Georgia, wracked by DTs, in a frazzled, paranoid state. Once I'd checked into a motel, I went to the liquor store across the street. It was just after 10am and already 94 degrees in the sun. I bought a bottle of Rebel Yell bourbon, some Coke, a bag of ice and a pack of Winstons. By mid afternoon, I'd drunk the bottle of Rebel Yell and the air conditioning had given me an ice cream headache. I went into the bathroom. I coughed. Something had been tickling the back of my throat. I spat a big blood-ball, fleshy and disgusting, into the sink. I coughed and a twin, misshapen and spotted as a crushed strawberry, followed. I lay down on the bed, scared. I woke up sometime around midnight. I was craving a drink again. I watched TV until dawn rose and then I fell asleep. By noon the following day, I was sucking on a bottle of beer, the blood-spitting a distant memory, something that had happened to someone else.

89

'That was close!' she said, laughing.

It was 1 am. I had arrived in Houston direct from Athens six days earlier.

I was in a jeep with a complete stranger.

'Tell me about it,' I replied.

She had just run a red light and nearly broad-sided a camper van.

She pulled into a 24-hour liquor store. I didn't even know her name.

'This OK?' she asked, holding up two sixpacks of cheap beer.

'Sure,' I said.

We got back in her jeep. I lit the cigarette that she had just flipped up to her mouth.

'Aaah,' she moaned. 'Sweet nicotine.'

We tore out of the parking lot, tyres screeching. She pulled into the traffic without even looking.

'Shit,' she said as we got hooted at by another mob of angry drivers.

She ran another red light.

'Hand me a beer will you?'

I pulled another can free, opened it and put it in her

hand. She was already ripped out of her mind. I had met her earlier that night at a party. We got back to her place. She had just moved in. The whole apartment was piled high with boxes. We drank a few more beers and then she asked me if I wanted to take a shower with her.

'Fuck that was good,' she said and took a hit off a lukewarm, half-drunk beer that had been waiting ever since we came out of the shower and devoured one another. We were lying wrapped up together in some sheets on the cheap, scratchy carpet.

'I know,' I said and kissed her.

She spat a mouthful of beer into my mouth. I wanted to ask her who she was, but it was already too late for that.

90

The bus was tearing through the middle of Iowa when they appeared on the horizon – thousands and thousands of tractors. I rubbed my eyes with the back of my hand. Still there. Brand new, shiny tractors. Rows and rows of them, as far as I could see, in lines, in formations, the symmetry perfect. I looked around the bus to see if anyone else could see them but everyone was asleep. The sun was coming up. I hadn't slept all night and thought the DTs were playing tricks on my mind. I'd picked up a connection somewhere in Arkansas around four that morning. I was travelling from Houston to Minneapolis. By 10am, the sun was wide awake. I was smoking a cigarette and sipping on a coffee that made my hands shake even more. The Greyhound depot was next to a drug rehab clinic. People with grey faces wandered the clinic lawns, plastic name-tag bracelets dangling around their bony wrists. They were on one side of the street, I was on the other. The announcer made a final boarding call for my bus. I threw my cigarette down. Iowa. Shakes. Shivers. Chills. Thousands of tractors . . .

91

My last year at university, I lived in a faded Victorian house on the Peckham–New Cross border with eight other Goldsmiths' students. Mike had moved in with his younger brother and, after breaking up with Laura, I was left estranged from her and most of our friends. I thought the neutrality of strangers would be a calming influence. My new flatmates turned out to be as damaged as I was: an anorexic, a speed freak, a stoner bulimic-nymphomaniac, a sports fanatic who burned himself whenever he got stressed out, two born-again Christians, a hypochondriac MA student and a bulimic fresher.

92

On the first night of the new term, I was staggering around the campus bar drunk to the eyeballs, looking for a familiar face, when I ran into Laura.

'Hi. How was your summer?'

'Good. And yours?'

The tension between us was taut, cheese-wire sharp.

'OK.'

Then there was awkward silence. And then we both said

the same thing at the same time, our mouths mirrors, reflecting back mutual feelings.

'You look good.'

We both laughed at the stereophonic statement. I didn't want us to start up again though.

'I've got to go now,' I told her. 'I've got a drink waiting.'

'You're still drinking then,' she said.

Nirvana's *Nevermind* was playing over the bar PA.

'Look, I've got to go.'

She grabbed the sleeve of my jacket.

'Fancy a quick fuck in the toilets?'

I wanted her. More than anything. But not like that.

'I've got a drink waiting. I've got to run.'

I didn't look at her or wait for her response. I pushed off into the crowd, my step heavy, reluctant.

93

Every Tuesday, I saw Veronica at 10 am. I always paced my drinking on Monday nights so I wouldn't sleep through the alarm clock. She and I hit a stalemate. Her words didn't work any more. She would tell me how ill I looked and repeat again and again that she thought I was an alcoholic but I didn't want to hear any of it.

'Why have you given up?' she kept asking me.

'I haven't,' I'd snap back.

'You have. Look at you. You've got another nasty cough. You look terrible. Why are you doing this to yourself?'

I was staring at my fingers. They were stained yellow from smoking too much.

'If I knew that, I wouldn't be here would I?'

Cheap wine boxes. A gift to the unrepentant alcoholic. I worked out that each one was equivalent to four bottles of wine. I started to stay in on Saturday nights. I'd settle in front of the TV at 5pm with a red wine box. I'd talk to other people in the house, about what was on TV, the weather, where they were going that night. They would go off to their rooms and get dressed up. When they'd all gone out, I would sit on my own, watching a film, filling my glass over and over again. It was slow drinking, slow suicide. I just sat there and sipped my wine, neither sober nor drunk. Eventually people in the house would start to come home. They would make snide comments about how I was still in the same faded armchair, still hooked up to my wine box like it was an IV drip. Midnight would tip-toe past. The first ones home would start yawning and then they'd go to bed. The others staggered through the front door, joining me for cigarettes, trying and failing to get me to give them a glass of my precious wine. By 3 am, they would all be back or in bed. I always knew that the fun was over when the last person came home. Sometime after, I would lean over to re-fill my glass and find that the box was empty. I learned all the tricks. I would rip open the cardboard box and take out the bag. If I squeezed really hard, I would be able to milk a final glass of wine out of that bag, the last drops of wine dripping into the glass like blood.

95

When I met Maria, I was lost in a twilight zone of promiscuity. Veronica had long since nailed this as just another symptom of what was wrong with me. Something had to change. I didn't want to go on like that. Maria was different. She didn't sleep around and she didn't like drinking. She had big blue eyes, long ratty dreadlocks and an array of piercings. She was already moaning about my drinking by our second date.

'Why do you have to get so drunk all the time?' she complained as we sat listening to Hole in my room, a growing mountain of crumpled beer cans by my side.

'Because it keeps me sane.'

It was my stock line by then, part of a well-rehearsed speech.

'Do you really believe that?'

She was closing in on the truth like an amateur Veronica.

'Maybe.'

'I think you're an alcoholic.'

She spat the word out like it was the most disgusting word in the English language.

'That's ridiculous.'

'I'm serious. You need to get help.'

I got up to flip the record over, the needle aptly stuck in a groove.

96

Veronica and I sat in silence.

'You're going to die if you keep this up.'

I told her that I'd thrown up blood again the night before. I felt like shit. I couldn't stop though. I couldn't find the trail of salt back to where it had all begun.

'What is behind all of this?' she said, exasperated.

I had missed our previous session because it came after a four-day binge. When the sports nut who was always burning himself got hold of a sack of magic mushrooms, all of us – bar the born-again Christians – took them. The night after, every one in the house took them again – cleaning his stash out. I got drunk on both nights too. So I was planning a quiet night in – with a wine box – when Paul turned up on my doorstep straight off a coach from Cardiff. He had a gram of speed with him which we ended up sharing. When he cleared off the next day, Mike came over with a bag of weed that his brother had given him. When I woke up on Tuesday morning, to the sound of my alarm clock swearing obscenities, I was too wrecked to go and see Veronica, so I just went back to sleep.

'I don't know. I don't know. I don't know.'

97

Maria kept harping on about my drinking and I got sick of it. I didn't want to spend all our dates talking about how much I drank. She had to go. She turned up one Saturday afternoon, rousing me from a filthy hangover. I'd been out shooting double vodka-Pernods with Mike the night before. She sat on my bed and said she was worried about me. She'd heard about my recent binge and was scared. She begged me to go to an Alcoholics Anonymous meeting. I laughed and told her to mind her own business. When she asked me to give her one good reason why I wouldn't go, I said, Because I'm not an alcoholic. She stormed off without saying goodbye.

Kim, the anorexic girl who lived in the basement, opened her door. I made some small talk about whatever film I'd been watching up in the lounge and then asked if I could talk to her. She invited me in and I sat down on her bed.

'Did you drink all of that yourself?' she asked, pointing at the empty bottle of bourbon in my hand.

'Yes,' I said. 'And I'm not even drunk.'

She had such a beautiful face. Her suffering had made a saint of her.

'What did you want to talk to me about?'

'That.'

I knew she got it because she was so out there herself.

'What do you want to do about it?'

Her cheekbones were sharp and tragic.

'I want to stop.'

We talked for a long time about my drinking and then she asked me if I wanted her to call AA for me. I said yes. I was ready.

We went up to the lounge. It was late, maybe 2 am. She found the number for AA in the phone book and dialled it. She handed me the receiver and left the room.

'Hello?'

'Hi, is this Alcoholics Anonymous?'

'Yes. How can I help?'

A gruff male voice. Stern, not that friendly.

'I have a problem with my drinking.'

'What's your name?'

'Nick.'

He told me his name.

'Are you drunk right now, Nick?'

'No. I drank a bottle of whisky tonight and it didn't even get me drunk.'

'Do you want to stop drinking?'

'Yes.'

'You need to come to a meeting then. Could you make a meeting this coming morning?'

Panic. Denial. If you do this, you can't drink any more. Quick. Do something.

'The earliest I could make is in the afternoon.'

'I would recommend that you go to a meeting as soon as possible.'

'But I can only make the afternoon or early evening.'

I could hear myself back-pedalling. I could hear the sudden terror in my voice. What was I doing? Alcoholics call AA . . .

'I can send a member of the fellowship to pick you up tomorrow at a quarter to four. Where are you?'

I gave him my address. It was too late. I'd said it. Now he knew. So did Kim. So did Maria. So did Veronica. So did everyone . . .

'Someone will come for you later this afternoon. Now try to get some rest.'

I thanked him and hung up. I lit a cigarette. There was no sound anywhere, not in the house, not outside. Everyone else was asleep.

99

'Is this Alcoholics Anonymous?'

'Yes it is,' responded a deep, smooth voice. 'How can we help?'

'Well, last night, things got out of hand and I called you.'

The hangover was brutal. It was the middle of the afternoon, sometime in early December 1991. I'd just woken up. I was starting to wonder just how sober I had really been the night before. Going down to ask Kim for help. Calling AA.

'Why did you call?'

'Well, I thought I was drinking too much and whoever I spoke to said that they were going to send someone around to collect me this evening and take me to a meeting.'

My voice was shaky. I tried to clear my throat.

'And?'

And? And I need a drink. And I don't want any of this AA crap. And I wish I'd never called.

'I don't need anyone to come around today. I'm fine. Can I just leave it please?'

Dead air.

'I'm fine, really.'

Not even the sound of his breathing.

'Thanks,' I said and hung up.

I went back upstairs to my room and opened a beer.

100

Two days into 1992, I was sitting alone in the lounge at my parents' house. I had the bottle of Rémy Martin that someone had given my father for Christmas beside me. It was empty. Earlier, I had been to a pub with Paul and drunk a couple of pints. Then I came home and drank the bottle of brandy, watching MTV.

'What the hell are you doing?'

My sister had just come home and stumbled in on my private party. She was still at school and still living at home.

'Watching TV.'

She shook the bottle.

'It's empty,' she said. 'You haven't drunk the whole bottle have you?'

'Why?'

'It's not yours!'

She sighed and went upstairs to get ready for bed. I crept into the kitchen and scooped up the bottle of Rebel Yell that I was saving for a special occasion. I took it into the lounge, tore the cap off and started drinking straight from the bottle. I was about a quarter of the way through it when the door swung open again.

'For god's sake! Go to bed!' my sister hissed, trying not to wake my parents who were sleeping above us.

'No,' I said, watching U2 play 'All I Want Is You'.

'What's that?'

'What?' I said, again ignoring her.

'That bottle.'

'It's a bottle of Rebel Yell.'

'Have you lost your mind?'

She snatched the bottle away from me. For a second, we were children again and it was one of those stupid games we used to play. She told me again to go to bed. This time I did. I staggered upstairs and into the bathroom. I squeezed toothpaste on to my brush. Half of it went into the sink. There were two, three, four, five toothbrushes. I was trying to figure out which one was real and which ones were imaginary when I spun round and vomited into the toilet. There was a lot of blood. Not just snotty red strings or specks. The water was red, like someone had emptied half a bottle of tomato ketchup in there. Oh shit, I thought. I'm going to have to stop drinking for a while.

'How do you feel sober?' she asked me.

There was relief on Veronica's face. Only now, a year into this, were we really getting somewhere. I hadn't touched a drop since seeing all that blood in the toilet. After yet more 'we're worried about the amount you drink' lectures from my parents and sister (and naturally, I told no one about the blood nor did I see a doctor), I side-stepped their concern by going cold turkey. When term began again, I researched stomach ulcers in the university library and discovered that they usually heal in six weeks. I figured that I had something similar, so I put a six-week deadline on my sobriety. Six weeks . . . and then I'd be able to drink as much as I wanted. By the time I was sitting in Veronica's office – two and a half weeks sober – the craving had cooled off and had now taken on the intensity of suffocating or drowning.

'Lost. Confused. Bored. Sick of not being able to sleep. Uptight. Angry. Agitated. Restless.'

'Why?'

'Because now my life is like a black-and-white TV. When I drank it was a colour TV. All the colour's gone.'

'Why do you need alcohol to make life interesting?'

Interesting? I need alcohol to breathe . . .

'Because it opens me up, gets rid of that stiffness, shuts all of that crap up.'

'And hangovers, bronchitis, vomiting blood. Those things are a fair exchange?'

'Of course not. I don't know what all that health stuff is about.'

'It's about wanting to hurt yourself.'

'Maybe.'

'Not maybe. It is. The drinking, the drugs. It's all a way to damage feelings that you find too painful to live with.'

She knew about the drugs. If only she knew about the cutting . . .

'I suppose so.'

'How are your friends treating you?'

'They're keeping their distance.'

'Why do you think that is?'

'They don't like me unless I'm out of control.'

'What makes you say that?'

'The facts. They're keeping me at arm's length.'

'Does that bother you?'

'It makes me want to drink again. I feel like I've done something wrong.'

'Which is?'

'Be myself.'

102

Laura and I collided in a pub next to campus. She asked me if it was true that I had quit drinking. I said it was.

'Damn you,' she scowled, her hand wrapped tight around a pint of beer. 'I put up with all that shit from you and now you go and sort yourself out.'

'I wouldn't say I've sorted myself out. I'm trying to.'

'You seem like you're doing really well. You've lost weight.'

I had. The pounds were just falling off me. Two packs of cigarettes a day, a lot of coffee, hardly any sleep.

'Do you want to come back to my place for a chat and some coffee?' she asked, smiling in her coy way.

I could picture Veronica shaking her head and pleading with me not to go.

'I don't know,' I said.

'Come on. Let's go.'

I wanted to say no but I couldn't. She made coffee and we sat on her bed talking. She got sentimental – something she never did – and opened a drawer full of cassettes. I could see my handwriting on dozens of tape sleeves.

'I still listen to all the tapes you made for me.'

She put one on. The album just happened to be one that had often played backdrop to our arguments. We kissed, fell into bed, made love, her tongue tasting of beer, her kisses getting me drunk.

103

On Valentine's Day, I started drinking again. I don't know what happened. It might have been the tangled emotions that came with loving Laura, it might have been the sterility of my new home in a hall of residence on campus for final-year students, it might have been the amount of course work I had, it might just have been because I stubbed my toe that morning. I spent almost an hour in a pub with Mike agonising over whether or not to have a drink. Mike's take on all this was that I should get a drink and see what happened. I kept thinking of what Veronica would say but I also kept looking at all the people laughing in the bar. It was like flipping a coin. One side was safe and sensible, the other reckless and seductive. When Mike slammed my tenth pint of beer down on the table – he and I were always keeping tabs on how many rounds we bought – I was 'normal' again. I was out of social exile, talking so much my jaw ached.

'It's Valentine's Day,' slurred Mike, his eyes rolling. 'Who do you love?'

I pointed at my pint of beer. Neither of us laughed.

104

A few weeks later, I ran into Maria in the campus bar.

'Why didn't you come and see me?'

I'd woken up two days earlier to find a note from Maria by my bed asking me to drop by.

'I've been busy,' I said, wondering why she was so angry.

'Busy? You bastard. You weren't too busy when you wanted to fuck me were you?'

She was furious. Her silver nose ring, catching an overhead light, blinded me for a moment.

'What? What are you talking about?'

My memory shrugged. It didn't have any answers either.

'Don't you remember?'

'Remember what?'

I remembered that she and I had gone out drinking, that we went back to my room to drink bourbon, that she couldn't handle her liquor, that she stayed over because she was too drunk to walk home.

'Us sleeping together the other night?'

I remembered getting into bed with her.

'We slept together?'

She looked at me. There were tears in her eyes.

'You don't remember do you?'

I didn't remember anything.

'You bastard! I fucking hate you!'

And then she walked away.

105

I got bronchitis again. I resented the antibiotics and still drank on them. Veronica was at the end of her rope with me.

'Everything was going so well for you. Why did you have to go and blow it?'

I had blown it. It was so easy to be drunk, to be out of control. I could be everything I wasn't when sober. I was deluded of course, equating alcohol with a better 'me'. Veronica, who had started to become more aggressive with me, snapped at this last session before the Easter break.

'You are an alcoholic. You're making the depression worse, the anxiety worse. You're wrecking your kidneys, your liver, your lungs, your heart. You've got bronchitis again. You come here and cough and splutter. Why can't you see what you drinking is doing to your health? You're killing yourself.'

I went home for Easter, relieved to get away from her for four weeks.

'Do you know who I am?' I asked Paul when I first arrived at the hospital.

He stared straight through me.

'It's me,' I said. 'Nick.'

No flicker of recognition, nothing.

'Do you know who I am?'

Still nothing. The first any of us knew about Paul's nervous breakdown was when his mother called and told me that he had been flown back from Spain and admitted to the psychiatric wing of the hospital I once worked at.

'I am Batman,' he said after a long silence. 'I am Batman.'

He spread his arms out like wings and began to run up and down the length of the ward. I watched him, arms outstretched, a maniacal grin on his face.

When I came home for Easter break, I went out on the first night back with Dennis and Paul, like we always did. Paul was wound up tight, fit to snap, but we thought that was down to the amount of coke, ecstasy and speed he'd been taking. He was also revising for finals, going on long runs every morning, planning to start his own travel company and making frequent trips to Madrid where he was screening reps for his business. He sat in the pub and talked us through a big fat business start-up plan. We had no idea what he was going on about.

'I am Batman!' he yelled every so often.

I tried to stop him by grabbing his arm whenever he passed me but he shook my hand off each time.

'I am Batman!'

He was now shouting it loudly enough for a nurse to

poke her head through the door. She hurried off and came back with an orderly who restrained Paul while she gave him a shot. All the colour drained from his face and he fell on to his bed, groaning and moaning.

They kept Paul in hospital for four months. He missed his finals – his mother had to defer his exams for a year. The medication wiped him out. He jumbled up his words, had trouble remembering anything and worst of all, got into a habit of drooling. As he came around, he became aware of where he was. I visited him almost every day for the rest of the Easter break. I cooled my drinking off. I didn't want to end up like that. Lost in one of those medication cages. Trapped in one of those breakdown palaces. I remember Dennis saying to me after we visited Paul together that he couldn't understand why Paul had cracked up. I always thought you were the one who was going to snap, he said, as we drove out of the hospital driveway. He was right. It should have been me . . .

Paul used to take me to the smoking room. The first time we went in there, a woman asked me if I would drive her to a Barclays bank. I didn't know what else to say, so I said I would. Then, every time a visitor like me, someone from 'out there' as she put it, came into the room she asked them too. Within an hour, she had four offers of a ride to the bank. Paul and I tried to talk but it was impossible. A man with wild white hair and a shaggy beard kept inter-rupting us and asking me if I could bring him some Guinness next time I visited Paul. A stick-thin girl, who couldn't have been older than sixteen, sobbed in the corner. I wanted to comfort her but it wasn't my place.

The patients started fights about everything – the nurses, the chairs, the weather – and every time I left that room, I thought I was going crazy too. I always thought the same thing driving home: how can Paul get better in a place where everyone is broken?

I was tired. I had cleared months of revision in a matter of weeks. I was going to sit my finals in less than a month. I plopped myself down next to Paul on his bed. He put his face in his hands. I didn't know what to say. The man in the bed across from us was masturbating. Paul got up and wandered over to a table between two beds.

'What about a game of scrabble?' he asked, pointing at a scrabble board.

'OK,' I said, hopeful that he was coming round.

He tipped the letters out. We pulled two chairs over to the table.

'You start,' I said.

'Hmmm,' he mumbled, pushing a tile or two around.

After some deliberation, he cleared the board of tiles.

'Are you going to start?' I said.

'I have started,' he said.

'But you haven't put a tile down yet.'

'Yes I have,' he said.

His eyes were glassy.

'I've put seven tiles down.'

The board was blank.

'Which letters?'

'Whichever ones you want,' he muttered.

'You've put down seven letters – do they make a word or are they just random letters?'

'It's a word.'

'Which word is it? It would help if I knew so I can think about what letter to put down next.'

He stared at me.

'I've told you,' he said, getting irritable. 'It's whatever you want it to be.'

107

The sun was streaming in the windows and picking out the highlights in Veronica's hair. It was our last session. My finals were over. I'd got through them by the usual method: I stuck a fourpack of Colt 45 in the refrigerator every morning and allowed myself that ice-cold reward when I finished each day's revision. Everything was closing down, I was about to move back to my parents' house.

'Why didn't you go to hospital and get stitches?'

Ten days earlier, there was a free drinks party at my hall, a customary farewell to those about to graduate. Mike and I got so drunk that I fell on to a wine glass that someone had left on the floor of my room. The glass had folded out like one of those nature documentaries that shows the speeded-up process of a flower in bloom, and the stem had punctured my knee-cap.

'I don't know.'

'But if there was that much blood, why didn't you do something?'

The drinking went on all night. When I fell on the glass, I soaked a towel through with blood. Then the bleeding stopped. And there was more free alcohol. The party ran on until the next morning. I got a few hours' sleep before the pain woke me. My knee was badly swollen. I couldn't walk on it. I had to get a friend to take me to hospital. A doctor took an X-ray of my knee and picked through the wound for fragments of glass. She said I was 'stupid' because the wound needed stitches but by the time I made it to hospital, it was too late.

'Look at you now,' Veronica said. 'You've got a terrible limp.'

I didn't care. I was just pissed off that I'd blown all the wild drinking days that I dreamed of during all those beer-rationed revision days.

'How do you feel about graduating?'

Butterflies in my stomach. No Sale signs in my eyes.

'I think I need to get out of this place.'

She ran a hand through her hair. There was nothing left to say.

Time was up.

108

New York was a sprawling mess. Sweltering heat. It was July 1992. I was fresh out of university and staying with my friend Jennifer for a week. She had gone to work and left me sleeping on her couch. I'd woken up hung over, taken a shower, gone out to get some brunch and then picked up a chilled sixpack of Coors. I spent the afternoon up on the roof of her apartment building, sunbathing, smoking cigarettes and drinking beer. All of Manhattan lay before me, smouldering, burning, choking. Everything looked so unreal from the thirty-ninth floor of a sky-scraper block. Cars became ants, people: specks of dust. I tried to imagine what it would be like to be a bird and fall and fall and fall . . . only to open my wings at the last minute and swoop back towards the clouds. Jennifer's room-mate, Annie, came home from work first. I was already working through another sixpack. She threw her bag down and frowned at the beer on the coffee table.

'Is that all you ever do?' she said. 'You're going to kill yourself if you don't slow down.'

I raised the can to my mouth in mock-theatrical fashion and drained its contents. I banged the empty can down on the table and sighed.

'Hi Annie,' I said. 'Good day at work?'

She waved her hand at me and vanished into her bed-room, slamming the door behind her. I smiled a sad smile.

109

It was my last night in New York. Jennifer and I got hammered at a bar on St Mark's Place with her boyfriend, Richard. We were heading back to her apartment in a taxi when I started to feel ill. I spent the next two hours throwing up blood in her bathroom. She begged me to let her take me to a hospital. I told her to forget it because it happened all the time and I was always fine the next morning. Eventually she grew tired of watching me retch and went to bed. When the alarm clock went off at 5.30am, she woke me up with a cup of coffee. She had booked me a cab to JFK so I could catch my early bird flight back to London. I staggered into the bathroom and vomited blood again. She insisted on making French toast for me. It'll make you feel much better, she kept saying.

I was in such a bad state that I couldn't even look at what

she'd made me, let alone imagine eating it. Every time she mentioned the word 'egg', nausea did a head-stand in my stomach. Eggs were all I could think about: egg yolks, egg whites, scrambled eggs, eggs benedict, poached eggs, fried eggs dripping in grease, boiled eggs that hadn't been cooked for the right amount of time, omelettes cooked in dirty frying pans, athletes swallowing raw eggs. When she pushed the plate closer to me, urging me to eat, I had to run to her bathroom to take a blood-flecked heave for the road. She got the message and wrapped the French toast in foil. She hugged me goodbye, stuffed the breakfast in my jacket pocket and waved me off.

What's the soft thing? asked one of the three security guards. I had set off the metal detectors at JFK. I had already emptied a pocket full of coins. Icy beads of sweat pushed their toboggans off my shoulders. Soft thing? Oh that, I said and took out the rectangle-shaped piece of foil. They shot glances at one another. Drop it in the bowl, growled the tallest of the guards. I did as he said. He unwrapped the foil. Inside: two pieces of soggy French toast. They laughed and waved me through.

The departure lounge was littered with cleaners. Everywhere I looked, mops were being dipped in buckets and dragged across floors. Arms, elbows and hands were sleepily operating brooms and carts. Industrial buffing machines were being swung from left to right, their hissing engines gliding just above the grime and the dirt. It was like watching ballet . . .

The stench of disinfectant made me nauseous again. No matter where I went, the smell followed me, clung to me. I paused by a large window and watched planes taking off. I took out a crumpled pack of Winstons. I was about to light up when I spotted the first of the endless no-smoking signs that surrounded me. I hadn't noticed them before. JFK was now a no-smoking airport. Shit. I struggled to get the cigarette back in the packet without snapping it because my fingers were trembling so badly. I sat down. The room started to spin. I got up, looked for the nearest toilet sign and moved fast.

I pulled the flush. The water came, hitting the bowl with the impact of a breaking dam. Or at least that's what it seemed like to me. To a normal person – a person not enslaved to DTs, a person who wasn't vomiting blood, a person who wasn't thinking that a cold beer would solve all of this, a person who wouldn't dream of getting on a seven-hour flight if they were vomiting blood – it would have just been a toilet flushing.

When the plane took off, I turned to the woman sitting next to me. She was in her forties: fresh faced, healthy skin glow, bright eyes, well-kept hair, nails, everything. She smiled. I looked away and pressed my head against the window. It was cool against my cheek. I imagined that it was a snowball melting in the cauldron of raw, burning pain in the pit of my stomach. My eyelids were heavy. We were in steep ascent. Barely off the ground. The Fasten Seatbelts lights glowed in authoritative red above every seat. The nausea got worse. I unfastened the seatbelt. Excuse me, I mumbled. The woman shifted her legs. I clambered over them. Two stewardesses told me to go back to my seat. I shoved past them, pointing at my stomach. I waved away their offers of a sick bag and stumbled into the toilet. There was more blood but not as much as before. Thank God for that . . .

I went back to my seat. Caught my breath. Buzzed for a stewardess and asked for a glass of milk. Feeling a bit queasy? she said, handing me a carton of milk. Milk had never tasted so vile, so overpowering. I sat back and closed my eyes. I let my head slump against the window. I was woken seven hours later by a violent landing, one of those landings where the plane bounces a few times before its wheels find the grip they're looking for. I rubbed my face. The woman next to me shot me a 'glad to see you're still alive' look.

110

Mike was the first to land a job. Three weeks after graduation he was hired by a shipping company as a trainee account manager. I was sending out hundreds of CVs and letters. Each morning over breakfast, I picked through a stack of form letters that all climaxed with the impersonality of a stamped signature. After a summer spent collecting unemployment benefit, I ended up working for a month in a record store before taking a job working nights and weekends with a telephone market research company in West London. The work was good for me – the structure, the focus. When I got back from New York, instead of seeing my doctor, I had put everything down to too many cigarettes and too much bourbon. I quit smoking as soon as I got off the plane and made a new drinking rule: no spirits, no lager, no bitter – just Guinness and wine.

Jane could tell I was in a bad way. My stomach was hurting again and my hands were trembling. I was over-weight. Dennis kept teasing me, saying I looked like I was five months pregnant.

'Are you OK?' she asked.

The shittiest February weather imaginable bore down on us.

'Sort of.'

I was on a sabbatical from the telephone job because I'd been hired as a temp on a six-week market research project for British Rail. I was working with another graduate – Jane – and our job was to ride the train from Euston to Birmingham and back, twice a day, seven days a week, interviewing passengers about how they rated the rail line.

'Another hangover?'

'Yup.'

I made a joke out of turning up for work everyday hung over.

'You look very pale. Do you feel all right?'

We were walking around Birmingham on a break.

'Not really,' I told her. 'I feel terrible.'

'Look, here's a sandwich place. Let's get something to eat.'

After eating, I felt better.

'You've got your colour back now,' she said. 'You had me worried for a minute.'

Another lunch time in Birmingham, Jane dragged me to see a palm reader who, aside from telling me things about my life that no one could possibly know, told me I was heading for a 'major emotional upheaval in autumn 1994'. She wrote this phrase down on a piece of paper which I glued into my journal, often staring at it when I was drunk and wondering what was going to happen to me.

112

Creak. I woke up with a jump. There was someone on the stairs. I put my bedside light on. *Creak.* There it was again. I'd gone to bed early because all day at work a savage hangover had been beating me with sticks. My parents and sister were away on holiday – I hadn't been away with them since I turned seventeen. I thought my mind was playing tricks on me. I hadn't drunk a drop of alcohol all night. I figured it was just another dose of the DTs. *Creak.* This time closer, louder. I threw back the covers and got out of bed. Whoever it is, I thought, is almost at the top of the stairs. Burglars? I grabbed an empty wine bottle – a relic from another night – from the window sill. Who's there? I yelled. Who is it? Silence. *Creak.* I crept to the door. I listened for a sound. Nothing. I pulled the door open, ready to swing the bottle like a bat, and ran the four or five paces through the dark to my parents' room. I heard the shuffle of footsteps and then the kitchen door rattled at the foot of the stairs. I locked the door behind me and, using the phone by their bed, called the police.

There's no one here, said one of the six police officers encircling me. They had arrived like a cavalry dispatch: a riot van, a squad car, blue flashing lights, torches, batons.

Someone was on the stairs, I said. I heard them. They shot each other coded looks. Are you alone tonight? asked the one in charge. Yes, I said and then realised what he was getting at. We've searched the house and the garden, he said. There's no sign of forced entry. Call us if you have any more trouble. I thanked them and they filed out to their vehicles. I sat down on the stairs. What now? Have I gone crazy?

I went into the kitchen, scooped up a wine box, grabbed a glass and went into the lounge. I sat down, poured myself a glass of white wine. I lifted it with a shaking hand and downed it with one quick twist of my hand. I kept filling it up. Four glasses of wine in as many minutes and my nerves stopped howling. I suddenly realised that the police hadn't checked the cupboard under the stairs. I ran and got a knife from the kitchen. With four glasses of wine in my body, I tore open the door, ready for anything. I waited for the surprise, the attack. Instead: nothing but a basket of potatoes staring back at me. I started to laugh, first under my breath and then out loud. Potatoes. I'm afraid of potatoes.

113

'Was this a good idea?' Laura asked, slurping her umpteenth glass of wine.

As usual, we had got back in touch after a spell of not talking. One of us always called the other, just when it seemed we were slipping away forever.

'Is it ever a good idea?'

We tended to meet up, have a good time, get drunk,

sleep together and then start arguing in the dead of night about whose fault it was that we broke up.

'I guess not,' she said and topped our glasses up.

'So why do we keep doing it?' I asked. 'You don't want to get back together. So what are these nights about?'

She giggled.

'Oh,' I said. 'It's just sex is it?'

She looked tired. It was all the drinking. She drank every night now too.

'Of course not,' she said and kissed me.

114

The drive down to Cardiff was long and arduous. To pass the time, I bought twelve cans of Guinness. I also had a Mediterranean cookbook, a pair of scissors and some adhesive tape with me. I have no idea where I got these things or why I had them with me. Dennis was driving. Paul, now back in Cardiff getting ready to re-take his final year, was throwing a party at his house that Saturday night. He wanted us to go. I was starting my first serious career job on Monday morning. I had taken a post selling advertising space for a business magazine. I was probably offered the job because I had been sober for twelve days when I went to the interview. This latest attempt at quitting was prompted, as always, by another blood-vomiting footnote to a period of excessive, abusive drinking. At the interview, I was centred and reliable, good-humoured and sharp and the interviewers – seduced by my performance – offered me the job on the spot.

For the entire journey, I drank and made mobiles out of

the pictures in the cookbook. By the time we were an hour into the trek, aubergines, quiches, soups, paellas, shrimp dishes and other such delights were swinging from the roof of Dennis's car. He egged me on while playing the same old James Brown song on repeat. Cars crawled past us on the motorway, faces staring in disbelief as a photograph of a lobster blew in the breeze. By the time we stopped at a service station for petrol, I had drunk eight cans of Guinness and I annoyed Dennis in the toilets by trying to piss on his new shoes.

We got to Paul's house sometime after 8pm. I had drunk all twelve cans of Guinness. We went out to a nearby pub for four or five pints. When the party started at closing time, I was too drunk to even hold a conversation. I got into an argument with Dennis about whether or not we were even in Wales. I kept insisting that we were in Scotland. He got irritated with me and we went into Dennis's bedroom to have a full-blown argument. It ended when Dennis discovered that there was a roof terrace outside Paul's bedroom windows. He said he wanted to move all the furniture out there – long since his established party trick.

We locked the door and spent the next two hours humping chests of drawers, bookcases, lamps, a desk, chairs and so on out through the windows. Passers-by in the street stood pointing up at this spectacle, which only made us work harder. When everything bar the bed was out on the terrace, we went back to arguing about whether we were in Wales or Scotland.

Eventually, we got bored and Dennis went back to the party. I grabbed a blanket and lay down on the carpet and went to sleep. There was a huge commotion sometime around dawn when Paul discovered where his furniture was.

'What's the problem?' I asked, barely conscious.

'My entire bedroom is out on the terrace and it's fucking raining!' yelled Paul.

I sat up.

It *was* raining, really pouring.

'So what?' I said and pulled the cover over my head.

115

In the good old days, on the great drinking nights, there used to be a point where magic took over the evening. I used to say it was like that strong-man game at a fair where you strike the target with a sledge-hammer and, if you're lucky, the bell rings and you win a prize. The bell rang at different times on different nights. Some nights it rang twice, some nights not at all. I always drank in the hope of making the bell ring. By this time, though, most of my drinking nights were the same: me, tired and un-healthy, repeatedly slamming that sledge-hammer down, the bell rarely, if ever, ringing any more.

116

It felt like an ego trip to have my own stapler, my own ruler, my own Tippex, my own box of elastic bands, my own Biros and pencils, my own filing cabinet, my own chair – one that swivelled – my own desk, even my own telephone. I'd made it. No more nights and weekends cold-calling abusive strangers for a market research phone centre. Now, I was a big-shot sales executive, with my £9,000 salary, my ninety-minute commute, my Next suit, my father's hand-me-down trendy-in-the-Eighties Yves St Laurent ties, my infinite responsibility, my expanding pub-lunch corporate-power-player waistline.

Really, though, all I thought about was how long until I could drink. When would I get home? When would I be free to start drinking? How much could I drink and still drive into work? How much drinking could I get away with and still go in and do the required day's work? If I was too hung over to do much at work one day, then I would taper off my boozing that night and show up fresh-faced and jittery the next day and so on. If I drank too little and turned up to work the next day in a state of minor withdrawal, then I made sure I had a beer at lunch time. If I had an especially bad hangover, then I also had a beer for lunch: sometimes two pints of Guinness, sometimes two and a half – I never strayed beyond this, though, for fear of getting busted for drinking and driving.

117

Week nights were all the same. Long, sad stretches of drinking alone. My parents in bed, my sister on the phone in her room. Me, in front of the TV, drinking red wine, watching *St Elmo's Fire* on video. I must have watched that film once or twice a week for the whole of 1993. I kept it a secret though. Like being an alcoholic, it wasn't something I wanted to get out.

When the magazine broke sales records – mostly thanks to me – the Group Publisher of our division organised a 'reward' dinner for everyone. He also invited the company's board of directors who between them oversaw two hundred magazines. By the time we got to the restaurant, I was already half cut because my sales team had been to the pub at lunch time and then to another pub after work. After countless glasses of wine and a dessert that I passed on, someone from Editorial started a food fight. Within seconds, food was flying in all directions. When a piece of tomato struck my white shirt, I grabbed a large jug of cream and flung it in the direction of the Editorial table. My perception of space and time, hopelessly wrecked by how drunk I was, caused my arm to catch on a full bottle of wine which tipped over and flooded the table. The jug's contents – now redirected – splattered the face of the cigar-puffing Group Publisher. It was a disaster that played out in slow motion. A collective forty-strong sigh followed, then torturous silence. Cutlery rattled. There was a lot of whispering. I staggered out of the restaurant and collapsed on the pavement outside. Cars whizzed by. I was so smashed I couldn't get up. I knew my parents were coming to collect me. I just couldn't remember when.

When I showed up on Monday morning, my manager laughed and said, 'My oh my, did we make a spectacle of ourselves!?' I waited for the 'Can you come into my office' speech but it didn't come. Instead I found myself at the centre of the company's gossip machine. People buzzed around me all day, asking me to re-tell the story, asking for details.

Strangers winked at me on the stairs, by the coffee machine. I was confused: my cream-chucking stunt had turned me into a company legend. The next day, I was given a pay rise and promoted to a higher position on another magazine. When I arrived for the first day of this new job, my new co-workers laughed about the cream-throwing, made me re-tell the story and then gave me a standing ovation.

119

A light rain was falling outside the lounge windows. The kind of late autumnal rain that comes and goes without a great deal of fuss. I wiped the last of many tears from my face. I didn't even know why I was crying. It came out of nowhere. Two empty wine bottles on the table beside me. Nobody home. My only company the sound of some stupid bird chirping outside. It was 2 am. I was due at work at nine. A dark velvety blanket lay sleeping over everything. I was the only one on the street who was still awake. All of the other lights had gone out one by one, the last disappearing sometime after 1 am. I was tired and melancholic, dwelling on old memories that I couldn't let go of. I picked up the third bottle of wine and held it up to the light. Three, maybe four glasses to go and then there wouldn't be a drop left. The clock ticked away in the corner, reminding me that I was wasting my life with the drinking thing. But it was too late already. I couldn't shake it off. I caught my reflection in the window and sighed. I'm still here. Sack of bones. Bloodshot eyes. Bloated stomach. Puffy face. No amount of alcohol can get rid of me. I re-filled my glass and poured it into my mouth, hoping something might change.

A few weeks later, I was finishing a second bottle of wine, alone in my bedroom, when the door swung open and my sister and mother burst in like the FBI in a bad made-for-TV movie. I spun around in my chair, a glass of wine – the evidence, the proof – in my hand.

'What?' I barked.

'We've got to talk,' my sister said. 'You're drinking too much.'

'No I'm not,' my slurring as usual contradicting me.

'You are,' added my mother. 'It's out of control.'

'And don't take this the wrong way, but you're getting fat and it doesn't suit you,' followed my sister.

Fat?

'Nick,' my sister said. 'You're drinking a ridiculous amount every night. It's not normal.'

I'd been caught in the act. A bottle of wine on the desk. A glass in my hand. Unhappy. Overweight. Sickly. They were right. I looked like shit.

'You're not to have any more wine tonight,' cautioned my mother. 'You've got to do something with your life. You can't sit in here night after night hiding away, drinking all the time.'

It was true. I rarely went out at night any more. If I drove anywhere, I couldn't drink . . .

Can you both leave now, please?'

They pulled the door shut. I topped up my glass. Fat? I stood in front of the mirrored doors on the wardrobe.

By winter 1993, I no longer drank to get drunk nor did I drink to medicate my problems. I only drank for one reason: to feel normal. I didn't enjoy drinking any more. It wasn't even fun. When I was sober, I wasn't myself. I felt like someone else. I vaguely remembered what I should feel like – my natural state – and when I drank I returned to this image of who I thought I was. It was a crazy inversion, a mystical process whereby my sober and drinking personalities had swapped identities. Once I drank to get away from myself. Now I drank to return to myself. The more I realised this, the more terrified I became of my drinking. I was always trying to quit, always trying to find a way to punish myself enough so that I would be shocked into dropping the habit and starting a new life. The problem was, as soon as I was sober, I missed myself. I was like a rabid dog chasing my tail under a hot sun, my whole life a circus of circles.

There'd been more blood. A lot of it. Like New York. This time I'd done the sensible thing and gone to see my doctor. He checked me over, asked me questions about drinking (all of which I deflected with lies) and then wrapped up our appointment, saying, 'You'll have to lay off all alcohol for six weeks.' No matter how much I tried to trick my body, by quitting smoking or drinking coffee or by staying sober for a few nights, I was able to drink for fewer and fewer consecutive nights before getting sick and spitting blood.

Usually, I ignored the spitting and carried on, until I vomited blood. And then, after a few nights of not drinking, I'd go back to my wine. I hadn't gone to see the doctor because I was worried about my health, though, I'd gone to see him because I was worried about not being able to drink.

123

'Who the fuck are you?' I whispered.

Five or six old men were standing around my bed, looking down on me. I turned my bedside light on and then they vanished. The DTs had my head clamped tight in a vice and the craving tightened it a little more each day. I had snakes in my elbows and ants in my knees. Each sober day was as long as seven drinking days. Time seemed perverse, sinister. I was paranoid and jumpy. At work, I thought everyone was talking about me behind my back. When I could get to sleep, I had nightmares of packs of dogs chasing me. And there were the hallucinations, the visitations from those creepy old men. My brain was overheating, smoking, steaming. One night, I went swimming to try and burn off some of the withdrawal. I swam lengths, stopping after each one to cling to the end of the pool and gasp for air. My body was almost bankrupt. I had a funeral in my blood, my arteries little white crosses in a field of green.

124

The pub. Drinking with Dennis. After I'd drunk five or six pints, I told him how angry I was that I'd slipped after only twenty-one days. I was meant to stay straight for six weeks, not three. He shrugged. He didn't even bother to try and talk sense into me any more. He'd done his stint as Good Samaritan. Nowadays, his apathy had retired him. As I walked home from the pub, eleven pints singing hymns in my belly, I cursed myself for slipping. I was frightened. Now I couldn't even go a month without a drink. I went home, opened a bottle of red wine and drank some more, slumped in front of the TV, needing the wine to make me forget how disgusted I was with myself for getting drunk in the first place.

125

I was back at the medical centre within two months after vomiting a scary amount of blood again. As always, the spitting, the minor vomiting of blood didn't bother me, but the big ones did. Same routine. Hi, me again. Poor doctor, his heart sinking every time he set eyes on me. More medication. Same pills as last time. Higher dose though. Plus some liquid medicine. Another dull game of doctor-and-patient tennis. His prying questions had me running all over the court. But I hit my answers back so hard that he only saw chalk dust. His ace: no drinking for ten weeks. Meanwhile, I was off work again too. My book of excuses was wearing thin. The flu. Food poisoning. Car trouble. Mystery stomach bug. I'd used them all up.

Ten weeks? I set my brain to work on defining his ban. Was that ten weeks, as in ten working weeks – fifty days? Or ten full seven-day weeks? Ten weeks. Two and a half months. Perhaps that would make more sense rounded down to two months. Now, is two months eight weeks? Or nine weeks? Let's say eight weeks. And eight weeks is fifty-six days. And fifty-six days is less than two months. And if you round that down, oh, we're talking about one month without a drink. Why was I making such a big deal out of that trip to the doctor? Piece of cake . . .

When an exact calendar month was over, I started drinking again. I had an ingenious ruse to justify this latest slip: from now on, I'd only drink on Friday and Saturday nights. The new regime kicked in. I swam most nights after work and never drank between Sunday and Thursday but then . . . every Friday and Saturday, out with Mike or Dennis, there was carnage.

126

At the start of 1994, I was promoted again, this time to an ailing monthly business magazine, based at a different office. It was weird. The more erratic my moods got, the more ads I sold, and the more ads I sold, the more I got promoted. No matter how fucked up I was, I kept getting promoted. It was a ridiculous endorsement of a ridiculous life. To 'celebrate', I let my weekend drinking rule slip.

127

'What are you doing?'

Caught red-handed. Me on the stairs in the dark with another glass of wine in my hand. My mother, eyes narrowed with sleep, sticking her head through a crack in their bedroom door.

'Nothing.'

I was so drunk that I had to work really hard not to sound drunk.

'You've had enough. Now get to bed.'

Enough? I don't know what that means . . .

128

A supermarket checkout. 6 pm. The woman behind me in the queue playing with her long, black hair. Her selection on the conveyer belt: milk, two bottles of Evian water, high-fibre bread, low-fat yoghurt, lettuce, cottage cheese, apples, bananas. I remember these details because I made a note in my journal about it. I watched my selection – six bottles of red wine and a few microwave dinners that always tasted like plastic – clink its way down the conveyer belt. When the cashier handed me the slip to sign, my hands were trembling so violently I had to fight to keep the pen between my fingers. I pushed down hard, the point of the pen almost tearing the paper. Two or so miles down the road, I wound the window down, ripped off my tie and drove on as fast as I could, cutting up one car after another until I was home and it was dark and I had sedated myself and was sitting alone in the dark, listening to the same sad song on repeat on headphones, drunk to hell, carefree, gone from here.

My mother became the main obstacle to a night's drinking. Her tendency to burst from their bedroom and catch me with a re-fill on the stairs was becoming a real problem. So, I came up with a cunning plan. I'd come home from work and drink a bottle of wine in front of the TV, talking with my parents and sister. Eventually, my parents would head up to bed and my sister would get on the phone with her boyfriend. I'd pretend to go up to my bedroom and listen to music on headphones. I'd wait until my parents' light went out and then I'd go downstairs. Everyone in my family took a glass of water to bed. So I'd creep downstairs, open a second bottle of wine, pour a glass and then fill a pint glass with water. I'd hide the glass of wine by my left side, so that it was shielded in the dark and then I'd hold the water glass in full view with my right hand. When my mother popped out of their bedroom, ready to catch me, I'd say, 'What? I just wanted another glass of water.' She would mumble something and go back to bed. Sometimes, I would get sloppy and leave the corkscrew lying on the counter top. 'Why did you open another bottle?' my parents would ask over breakfast. 'When did you drink it?' After several of these interrogations, I took to hiding empty wine bottles in my wardrobe and then dumping them at the weekends – in recycling bottle banks – when my parents were out shopping.

130

'What are we doing up here?'
Dennis, like me, was soaked to the bone.
'I have no idea.'

We were standing on the steps of the Sacré-Coeur cathedral. All of Paris below us. Lights. Candles burning brightly. Silly flames. Attention-seeking golds and don't-look-at-me yellows. We'd arrived in Paris that morning for a weekend break, having drunk ten pints the night before and soothed our red eyes with breakfast bloody Marys at Heathrow. We walked all day, stopping for a drink here, a drink there, before splitting two bottles of red wine for dinner. Then the rain came.

What drew me to the Sacré-Coeur? I can't really say. There was a strong pull though. A tug in my gut. I had no idea where I was leading us and yet I knew exactly where I was leading us. Past the whores in Pigalle, past the smoky bars. Raindrops clung to the tips of our noses. The climb to the cathedral nearly killed me. But when we got there, the cathedral door was welcoming. I stepped inside. Incense. The candles. The Mass in full flow. The choir. The scale of everything. Heads bowed. Prayers, wishes.

A need for forgiveness throbbed in my neck. I was wet with shame. I knew I had to stop. Or it would stop me. I didn't want to die. I just wanted peace of mind. My eyelids were heavy. My head dropped forwards. I could have been anywhere. Far away. Floating. Daydreaming. I started to pray. I was surprised by this. Shocked even. I cut a deal. A plea deal. I promised to change my whole life if God – whoever, whatever – helped me to stop drinking. I prayed for a long time. There were so many things that I wanted to confess. Sins. Repentance. And then, when I was all talked out, the tears came. When I went back outside, I found Dennis hanging over the railings, smoking. We walked in silence back to our hotel. I knew he had seen me. Face in hands. Shoulders heaving. Penitent fool.

The next day. 5pm. Happy Hour at Harry's Bar. Long Island Iced Tea cocktails. More drinks at Café Deux Magots. Cocktails at a club in the Latin Quarter. Dennis and I spent £250 on drinks that night. The contract I signed at Sacré-Coeur was torn up and thrown in the gutter. In the early hours of the morning, we were drinking with some French women. I bought a round of cocktails. I climbed up on to the leather couches, trying to sneak behind Dennis and return to my seat. God knocked me off my feet. I splattered across the table. I was winded but all I cared about was keeping a tight grip on the drinks. I didn't spill a drop. I hurt my back but all five cocktails remained just as they'd been poured.

When I got home, the wine kept flowing. Every single night. No let up. The party was never ending. I forgot all about the Sacré-Coeur. My bottoming out. My confession. Then, once more, pathetic and repetitive: blood in the toilet bowl. Streaks. Blobs. Strings. I saw a message written in blood: stop this before it's too late. I went to see the doctor. This time, he stared searchingly at me and asked me if there was 'something' he should know about. I shook my head, neglecting to tell him that I could no longer even drink unless I had the following to hand: a sachet of Resolve, a packet of Rennies, a pint of milk, an over-the-counter prescription for maximum strength Gastrocote, antacids. I was medicating myself to prolong my drinking life. He told me again that I shouldn't drink for 'at least ten weeks' and gave me another prescription for the various medications that would calm down the inflammation in my oesophagus and stomach.

133

June 1994. Mike had organised a reunion. We met at a pub in New Cross. The one next to Goldsmiths. The one I had drunk in for three years. Standing at the bar, it was hard to ask for a tonic water.

'What's that?' asked one supposed old friend after another.

'Toxic Water,' I said, making fun of my situation.

I found these nights easier too if I pretended that soft drinks were the drinks I'd rather be drinking. Ginger ale was Jack Daniels, bitter lemon a margarita, cranberry juice a glass of red wine, lemonade a glass of white wine, Coca-Cola a rum and a coke, tomato juice a bloody Mary and so on.

It was one thing for me to deal with not drinking. Quite another for my friends to. Their mourning took the form of endless drinking stories.

'One night when we were in here, Nick threw up all over the table we were sitting at,' said Mike, slurring. 'It was that table just through those doors by the jukebox. He'd drunk eleven pints with eleven shots of Jack Daniels. Everyone stared at him because it was a Saturday night and packed in here. Then he got up, walked out of the pub. I followed him, thinking he wanted to go back to my place because he felt so ill. Instead he walked straight into the wine bar over the road and ordered a bottle of red wine. When I asked him about the puking up, he just shrugged his shoulders and poured us both a glass of wine. It was nuts!'

I missed me too. I was staying in a lot, watching TV, watching videos, playing guitar. I was swimming two, three nights a week. I was burying my head in a lot of work, using it as a distraction. I'd been promoted again to another monthly magazine based in a new office in West London. My ad manager had graduated from Goldsmiths at the same time as me. He had been on Laura's course. They knew each other. Outside work, I was going out on long bicycle rides, trying to clear my head. I was sick of getting sick. I wanted it to stop. I hadn't made any big decisions though. I hadn't quit drinking as far as I was concerned. I was just giving my body the time it needed to heal. I believed that once I was better, I would be able to go back to drinking like I did in the old days.

Mike finished another story. Everyone was doubled over with laughter. I wasn't listening. Sobriety gave every part of my life a surreal glaze. Watching them get drunk was odd. They seemed stupid, loud, irritating. I felt boring, estranged from the 'me' in the stories that Mike was telling. I pulled a cigarette from a pack on the table.

'What are you doing?' Mike asked, a part of him thrilled to see me screwing up again. 'You haven't had a cigarette for two years!'

I put it between my lips, lit it, inhaled . . . and within forty-eight hours, was back on twenty a day.

One day followed another until I was six weeks sober. I stuck it out. I was relieved when my stomach stopped hurting. I was relieved when the nightmares stopped. I started to see waking up in the morning without a hangover or that permanent grogginess as something good. I went swimming and cycling as often as I could. I kept channelling the craving, the anger, the frustration into exercise. Burning it out of me. Using the pool or open roads to listen to my emotions, to try to digest what I was feeling. I shed fourteen pounds in the first six weeks. Everything was paring down. There was a feeling that I was coming out from under a rock after a long, long sleep. I could concentrate. I was able to focus at work. I started reading again. I hadn't read a novel since I graduated. My appetite whetted, I binged on books. Jeffrey Eugenides's *The Virgin Suicides*. Jean-Paul Sartre's *Nausea*. Jay McInerney's *Brightness Falls*. J.D. Salinger's *Raise High the Roof Beam, Carpenters*. Reading brought back an avalanche of memories. School. Elizabeth. The library. My gap year. Laura. Exams. Veronica.

Early September. More than three months sober. My sobriety on auto-pilot. I was now the ad manager of the magazine – my Goldsmiths comrade had gone back to university. I was responsible for three members of staff and an annual turnover of £400,000. I was told that, at the age of twenty-three, I was the youngest ad manager in the company's history.

'Let's go and get a bottle of wine.'

I was sitting with Maria in her flat in Hackney. She had called me the night before. We hadn't seen each other in over a year.

'Don't be stupid!' she said. 'You've just spent an hour telling me how you've been sober for 112 days and how much better you feel!'

I wanted a drink. The craving was gigantic, bigger than oceans.

'Who cares what I said? I'm through with this. It's so fucking boring.'

And that was that. No one could have stopped me.

When I drank the last of the wine – Maria was sipping cider – I sat back in the sofa and realised what I'd done. For the first few sips, there was a flash of that old giddiness, ecstasy, that holy anaesthetic. But then it vanished. It was like I picked up where I'd left off. This bottle of wine followed the bottle of wine I'd had the night before: the 112 nights in between were erased. All that hard work, crushed and flattened beneath the enormity. Of my need. Of my hunger. Of my thirst. I had to have it . . .

The wine slung its noose around my neck. I said I needed to go to the toilet. I couldn't stand her looking at me that way any more. I went upstairs and locked myself in her bathroom. I looked for a razor blade. I saw a pink disposable razor by the taps of the bath. I picked it up. I hadn't cut myself in a long time. I couldn't even re-member the last time I'd done it. The urge returned.

Magnified. Amplified. I was shaking. I wanted a Rothko painting on my arm.

KNOCK. KNOCK.

'Nick? Are you OK? You've been in there for ages.'

I put the razor back on the bath tub.

'Hang on.'

I opened the door. She looked worried.

'What were you doing?'

I stared blankly at her. I had no idea.

137

I went to see a film – *When a Man Loves a Woman* – about an alcoholic who cracks up and quits drinking. I made a long journal entry that night about how much I identified with the character. When she says something about 'needing to learn to live in reality' once she's sober, I knew exactly what she was talking about. I had no idea how to live in reality. I was still angry with myself for slipping at Maria's place. I'd gone through another severe withdrawal. Back at work on Monday morning, another ad manager who sat behind me asked me what I'd done at the weekend. I told him I'd been to see the film.

'Oh right,' he said. 'I heard something about that on the radio this morning.'

He eyed me suspiciously. 'I think the penny's starting to drop.'

'About what?'

'You know,' he said smirking.

I lit a cigarette and buried my head in paper.

In early October, Maria called to tell me that she was about to move to Philadelphia for a year to work as an *au pair*. She said she wanted to see me before she left. I suggested that we drive down to Bournemouth, spend a night in a hotel, go for a midnight walk along the sea-front.

'I'm glad you're not drinking,' she said, as we tore down a stretch of open motorway.

'Really?' I said, unsure what I thought about it.

We checked into a hotel and then went downstairs to the bar. I was going to order a toxic water but my veins staged a revolt and stole my mouth long enough to make it say, 'A double vodka with grapefruit juice please.'

'Oh no,' Maria said. 'Not again. You said that after what happened the last time you saw me, you were never going to drink again.'

The barman set about fixing the drink. I ignored her. What did she know?

'Have you gone crazy?', she said.

'Yes,' I answered.

I didn't care any more.

By 10 pm I'd drunk a lot but I wasn't drunk. I just felt normal again. I was mid-way through a pint of beer when a cold sweat ambushed me. Everything went black for a split-second. I lost consciousness. It was like taking a little nap.

'Are you all right?' I heard her saying as I came back.

'I need to go to the toilet.'

I stood in front of the mirror. I was dripping with sweat and my skin was grey. Waves of nausea. Stabbing stomach pains. The ground moving beneath my feet. I splashed cold water on my face and went back to the table.

'Better?' she said.

'I'm fine. I don't know what that was all about.'

She looked frightened.

'Let's go back to the hotel,' she said. 'You've had enough to drink.'

I felt better once we hit fresh air and I told her that I thought the beer I'd been drinking was off and that it upset my stomach. I used this absurd excuse to convince her to join me in the hotel bar where I went back to what I knew worked: double vodkas with grapefruit juice.

139

Two weeks later, I got drunk for the last time. Chianti drunk. My mouth was stretched in a grimace so tense that my jaw hurt. The sky had the colours of a funeral. It was Sunday 23 October 1994. Freezing cold and depressing. It was my mother's birthday. I pointed three bottles of red wine at myself like they were loaded guns. I watched the wine sigh in the glass like blood. The Chianti picked through my brain like a mortician. Faulty circuits lay lifeless. Loose cables were limp and colourless. When the mortician was finished, my eyes were black as death.

140

I woke up dead on Monday morning. I had a glass of Resolve for breakfast. I couldn't face eating anything. I went to work. I smoked and drank coffee all day, hoping to override the hangover. That night, I didn't dare drink. I was too sick. I went to bed early and, for a change, slept straight through the night.

141

On Tuesday, the hangover was even worse. I was trapped in the hangover version of *Groundhog Day*. I sat at my desk, chain-smoking. One person after another came over to ask if I had the flu. No, I'm fine, I lied on auto-repeat, until it was time to go home. Sometime after 8 pm, as I sat in front of a re-run episode of *Thirtysomething*, the DTs came with their baseball bats and knives and chains and clubs. It started with twitches in my legs and arms. The floor sliding one way and then the other. The TV screen got blurry. There were heart palpitations. Icy beads of sweat dribbling down my sides. Teeth clenched. A seizure in my shoulders. Clammy palms. A spasm in my left leg causing it to spring up into the air. The chair I was sitting in shrank. The TV looked no bigger than a matchbox. My lungs were sticky. I put my head between my knees. Trembling, shivering. Burning up. So hot. I held my hands out. They were shaking like plates in an earthquake. I bit down on my tongue. I pressed my feet hard against the ground, one hand gripping the armchair, the other tugging at my lips, scratching my cheek, rubbing my nose. My father came into the lounge. He asked me if I was OK. I told him I needed a glass of wine. He got angry.

'You're ashen,' he said. 'A drink's the last thing you need.'

My mother walked in, took one look at me and knew something was very wrong. She asked me what the matter was. I tried to explain what was happening. They looked at each other, as if to say, What is he talking about? She told me to go to bed. When I stood up the room spun round until my parents looked like horses on those fairground rides. I went upstairs and sat on my bed, again putting my head between my knees. My mother lay a damp cloth across my forehead and stuck a thermometer in my mouth.

'What's wrong with me?' I asked as soon as she took the thermometer out.

'I don't know,' she said. 'I'll be back in a moment.'

Every part of my body turned numb. I was drifting in and out of consciousness. There was a moment of intolerable pain and then I thought I was going to pass out. Then, out of nowhere, hallucinations. Beautiful blue birds, everywhere, against a misty backdrop of autumnal sky. Hundreds and thousands of blue birds flying in slow motion. Passing over a black lake. That was all I could see. Not my bedroom or the desk or the chair or the stereo or the bedside drawers or the mountain of CDs and records or the overflowing bookcase. I snapped out of it. I saw myself in the wardrobe's mirrored doors. Pale, sweaty, shivering. Then the nausea came. Bile spilled into my mouth. I ran on rubbery legs to the bathroom. I got there just in time. Blood again. All over the toilet bowl. All over the toilet seat. Dangling from my chin. A string of bloodied something that looked like spaghetti clung to the side of the bowl. There were so many kinds of red: cherry red, tomato red, raspberry red, strawberry red, sunset red, bloody Mary red. I cleaned up and flushed the toilet.

'What's going on?' I heard my mother call.

'I just threw up,' I called back in a voice shot to pieces from all the vomiting.

I cleaned my teeth and splashed cold water over my face

and then opened the bathroom door. My mother was standing there.

'Are you OK?' she said.

'Not really,' I told her. 'I just vomited blood.'

142

The next morning, I got up for work like nothing was wrong with me. There was no question of me going to see a doctor. Ten weeks blah blah. I knew the drill. I was scheduled to pick up one of the sales executives who reported to me from a station close to work and then we were going to drive to Birmingham for an exhibition.

'Are you all right?' he asked as he got into my car.

'Yes, why?'

I had to keep pretences up. I was – after all – his manager.

'You look peaky.'

'Do I?' I said, in a matter-of-fact tone, releasing the hand-brake. 'I feel fine.'

Less than five minutes of silent driving later, I had to pull off the road.

'Why are you stopping?'

I slammed on the brakes and threw my car door open. I leaned out of the car and threw up on the tarmac.

'Jesus Christ,' he said, his voice faraway and fuzzy. 'Are you OK?'

I motioned to him with my hand to shut up. I vomited a second time. Then I hit the retching stage. More blood, shining on the tarmac in the crisp sun of the October morning.

'Gary,' I said, sitting back in my seat.

'What?'

'I'm going to have to go home.'

'You need to see a doctor.'

I need a drink.

'Can you pass me my cigarettes?'

'Cigarettes?' he said, astonished. 'Is that really a good idea?'

'I guess not.'

I drove back to the station and dropped him off.

'Will you see a doctor this morning?'

'Maybe.'

Of course I didn't.

143

I lay awake all night shivering and shaking. I was sweating so badly that at one point I had to go to the bathroom and towel myself down. It was disgusting – like I'd just stepped out of a shower during summertime in New York. As soon as I towelled myself down, I was soaked again. Once I was back in bed – after the second trip to the bathroom – my body temperature dropped. Soon I was freezing cold: teeth chattering, legs twitching, chest wet, doubled up with stomach cramps. I curled up in a ball, desperate for the pain to stop, my eyes snapped shut. Birds. Beautiful blue birds. Take me with you.

144

I was so sick on Thursday morning – and I went into work again – that I had to leave an hour after I got in. One of the other ad managers followed me into the kitchen as soon as I arrived.

'Nick,' he said. 'I think I should take you to hospital. You need to get checked out. You look like crap.'

'I'm fine,' I said, not sure if I was trying to convince myself or him. 'It's just a stomach flu I can't shake off.'

An hour later, after almost blacking out in the office, I was home, having driven all the way with double vision. I was shaking so severely when I got home, that my mother took me straight to the medical centre. My usual doctor was fully booked so I saw another doctor. He told me I had acute gastritis, prescribed me an anti-nausea drug and an anti-acidity medication and then asked me how much I drank. I said a few glasses a night. He said that was hard to believe because I was suffering from a textbook case of DTs. I asked him what he could do about it. He said there was nothing that could be done – other than me stopping drinking. I took the prescription and walked.

145

'I think I have a brain tumour.'

Three days later I was back at the medical centre. My doctor – my old, regular doctor – frowned. I told him I'd been in bed ever since I saw the substitute doctor and that I'd been having headaches, bad enough to convince myself that I had a brain tumour. He shone a torch into both of my eyes and asked me various questions. At the end of this mini exam, he told me that no, I didn't have a brain tumour. I'd seen far too many Woody Allen movies to take a doctor's evaluation at face value. I asked how he could tell. He laughed and told me that I had nothing to worry about. I didn't tell him that I also thought I had stomach cancer, lung cancer, AIDS, leukaemia and just about every other life-threatening illness I could think of. He gave me a thorough physical exam. He also asked me this time if I smoked pot or took any other drugs. I told him I didn't. And it was true, I hadn't smoked a joint since I left university. He gave me a stronger anti-acid medication that he assured me would clear up the stomach problems. He asked me again about drinking. Again I blocked his bid to make me accept the truth. He had no choice but to buy it: if I wouldn't face it then there was nothing he could do about it. He asked me if I thought that the depression had come back. I said I didn't think so, telling him that it was the opposite: I couldn't calm down.

'Come back in ten days', he concluded, throwing his hands up in the air. 'If you're still having problems.'

146

When I asked my mother where the ultra-violet sun lamp was, she looked at me like I'd gone crazy – do you blame her? I'd gone back to work. I think she hoped that that would put an end to all my weirdness. She asked me why I wanted it. As a child, I used the sun lamp – black goggles clamped over my eyes – to try and drain blocked sinuses. I said I wanted to give myself a suntan. So, resigned, bemused, she told me where it was. I went upstairs, found it, set it up, plugged it in. I was so sick of seeing my pale, sickly face in the mirror that I figured that if I used the lamp to give myself a fake suntan, then at least I'd only feel ill rather than look ill too, and then perhaps, if mind really was able to triumph over matter, then I'd be healthy again.

147

I read an article about stress in one of the Sunday newspapers and wondered if I was simply stressed out. The article recommended vitamins and supplements which might fight stress. I went to a supermarket and bought a basket full of stuff: Kalms (to help me relax), zinc (to combat depression), ginseng (to strengthen my immune system), iron (for fatigue), a big bunch of bananas (because the article said that bananas boosted the brain's serotonin levels). Then, that afternoon, I went running. I was out of breath before I even reached the end of the street but I pushed myself, convinced that exercise would help. After a bath, I sat in front of the UV lamp. I was rattling with pills, full of bananas and my legs ached from the run. Regardless, the sweats drenched me throughout the night and the pain in my stomach was worse than ever. The whole time, all I kept thinking was that there was only one reason for getting better: so I could have a drink and put an end to all of this.

148

'You have to get to the emergency ward at this hospital,' said my doctor, pointing to the name and address. 'You know where it is don't you?'

I nodded. I could see two of him. At 7:30 am I'd stood

over the toilet bowl, staring at what I'd soon know to be 'black stools', a symptom of internal bleeding.

'Here,' he added, thrusting an envelope into my hand. 'And when you get there . . . and I've called ahead so they know to expect you . . . give this to the receptionist.'

'Now hurry,' he said, his voice pink with panic. 'The bleeding can become quite profuse and you must be under medical supervision if that happens.'

He held the door open.

'One last thing,' he said as I turned to leave his surgery. 'Whatever you do, don't drive yourself. Did someone bring you here?'

'No. I drove myself.'

I hadn't mentioned the 'black stools' to my parents. He pulled a face of disbelief.

'Listen, please call someone and have them take you to the hospital. It's too dangerous for you to drive yourself.'

149

Traffic backed up all the way into a black sky. My knuckles white against the bone. Fingers strangling the steering wheel. It's too dangerous for you to drive yourself. When I get there I know what they'll say. You can never drink again. Sobriety. Forever. It's too dangerous for you to drive yourself. My head swimming. Cars reduced to smears of colour. I think of all the things that could go wrong: I could run out of petrol. I could break down. A tyre could blow out. The engine could overheat. Someone could crash into me. It's too dangerous for you to drive yourself. Teeth chattering like castanets. My heartbeat irregular and sick. My hands trembling. I wind the windows up and press a cassette into the stereo. Turn the music up. Wait to warm up. It's too dangerous for you to drive yourself. The last mile. Tropical heat. Windows steam up. I wind the windows down. Turn the heater off. Kill the stereo. Thoughts swirling. Flickers of death. Tiny blackouts. Blurred vision. I pull my shirt sleeve up. Sink my teeth into my left arm. Tight as I can. I could draw blood if I wanted to. The pain wakes me up. I can see the white line. It's too dangerous for you to drive yourself. I pull into the hospital car park. I stagger to the ticket machine. Pump the coins in. Tear off a ticket. Lock the car. Hurry. The gravel crunching beneath my feet. I could lie down on the ground. Double vision. Electric doors. Accident and Emergency. A fog of lights and beds and screams. Drugs and nurses and sunken cheeks. It's too dangerous for you to drive yourself. Reception. I queue. Legs like treacle. I wipe a stream of sweat from my forehead. I'm so cold my bones want to split. Shirt stuck to me. I hand the letter from the doctor to the woman behind the desk. 'Oh yes,' she says. 'We've been expecting you.'

150

Doctors, nurses and porters buzzed around me. I shivered in the skimpy sky-blue hospital gown. The pain in my stomach excruciating. Scissors, needles and pins limbo-danced beneath my ribcage. A nurse wrote my name and date of birth on a clear plastic bracelet and fastened it around my wrist. She handed me consent forms and a pen and asked me to read through the conditions and sign at the end. I got to the part about what happened if I died in their care and shut down. I signed my name on the last page. Another nurse wheeled in an intravenous drip and started to slap my left hand.

'Where have all your veins gone?' she joked.

She slipped the thorny needle into the back of my hand, attached it to the drip and a cold saline fluid began to ooze into my bloodstream.

'I'm really scared,' I said.

She smiled and then jabbed me with another needle and took a blood sample.

'Am I going to die?' I asked as my blood mushroomed in the syringe.

'No, you're not going to die.'

She disappeared behind the curtains, leaving me alone on the trolley bed.

A male doctor appeared with a nurse and began the routine examinations. I felt like a dying dog, being jabbed and stabbed and poked and prodded. There were no words left inside me. I just growled when they touched a part of me that hurt.

Next, a female doctor saw me alone. She had a kind face and so many questions that I didn't want to answer.

'How much do you drink each a day?'

'A bottle of wine on average,' I lied.

She didn't query what I said. She wrote down some comments on a photocopied form that was clipped to a chipped clip-board.

'Do you smoke?'

'I gave up a fortnight ago.'

No comment.

'I haven't had a drink since then either,' I added.

Still no comment.

I hadn't slept much either.

'Are you still taking antidepressants?'

I wish.

'No.'

'Since when?' she probed, not even raising her head from the clip-board.

I stared at her. She looked up.

My memory was shot to pieces.

I couldn't remember.

151

My parents were sitting by my bed when I came round. Earlier, I had been taken down to surgery for an exploratory endoscopy. I gagged when they sprayed a local anaesthetic on the back of my throat so they gave me a general anaesthetic. When they shot me up, it was heaven.

'How do you feel?' they asked.

The anaesthetic was wearing off.

'I wish I hadn't woken up.'

152

A group of student doctors flocked around my bed. A specialist ran through his diagnosis. Internal bleeding. Oesaphagitus. Gastritis. Duodenitus. One bleeding ulcer. One weeping ulcer. High blood pressure. Mild anaemia.

There were other things too but I stopped listening. I knew what was wrong. I knew what had caused all this. When they finally left me alone, I turned on my side and faced the wall, the hospital pillow rough against my cheek.

153

'Why have you done this to yourself?' the nurse asked as she stood at the foot of my bed, shaking her head.

'I don't know,' I replied, and I didn't.

My voice was hoarse.

She shuffled back to the nurses' station.

A dim light shone from the end of the ward.

Why had I done this to myself? What was 'this'? Drinking enough to get hospitalised? Drinking enough to almost kill myself?

154

The ward was silent apart from the sound of a respirator pumping the man in the next bed's lungs for him.

Just before I fell asleep, a simple thought. I don't want to die.

Not now.

Not tomorrow.

Not ever.

PART TWO

1

For me, drinking was a cure for an illness. Then it became an illness that needed a cure. By the time I was admitted into hospital, my life was a Catch 22. If I stopped drinking then the depression was unbearable. If I drank then the drinking was unbearable. I was boxed into a corner. There was nowhere left to go.

At best, depression is a gift, a chance to see life down-side-up. At worst, it's a curse, an illness that drains life of all colour and wonder. I was terrified of facing it head-on without my bag of tricks. I knew that I would run out of ammunition eventually. I knew my weapons would be taken away. I just didn't know when.

It was time to live or die. I had no other choices, no other escape routes. I had used up all of my drinking lives. All the self-medication formulas were of no use to me now. I knew where I had to go. I knew which path I had to follow. I knew I had to take a deep breath and start over. And I wanted to live. I knew this much.

2

When I got out of hospital, my stomach stopped hurting immediately. I went to see my doctor, told him the truth about my drinking and he referred me to an alcohol counsellor. He helped me confess my alcoholism to those close to me. My friends supported me all the way. I went back to work, but only after coming clean about my situation to my boss. He was understanding and told me that I could take time off whenever things got too much. He knew that it was going to be hard working in an office alongside two magazines dedicated to the wine and spirits trade: all those bottles being opened, all those wine tastings, that special whisky issue. The I went to my first AA meeting. It was like finding a second home. I clicked with the 12-Step Program and followed their recommended 90 Meetings in 90 Days master plan. I found a remarkable sponsor and we started to work through the 12 Steps, one by one. It was a time of miracles and wonder, joy and renewal. Finally, it was all over, in the past, conquered, done with, history.

Stop.

It wasn't like that at all.

I'm lying again. This time to you.

3

Dead air clung to both of our phones.

'A stomach ulcer?'

The Publisher, my boss, didn't believe me. I could hear it in his voice.

'Yes. A stomach ulcer.'

Silence. Two men breathing down telephone lines.

'If you don't come back soon we're going to have to re-think your position.'

What a dream.
'I know.'

4

I went to see my doctor for a check-up. He recommended that I see an alcohol counsellor. I told him I didn't want to. I was high on the arrogance of my denial. My addiction had made a martyr of me. My distress had become a crown of thorns. I didn't want to lose my hair-shirt, my identity. I was stubborn and sick. My mouth was defiant and clever. The trees were skeletons. The air was a grey whisper. Forever: a big word, bigger than me.

5

The attacks came once an hour, every hour, regardless of where I was or what I was doing. Bright, electric, demented. They'd been so bad since I left hospital that I'd gone back to see my doctor twice since my first check-up. I was always there. We were getting to be good friends. As usual, I gave him an elaborate roll-call of symptoms.

Breathlessness
Dizziness
A sensation that the floor was moving beneath me
Blurred vision
A racing pulse
Heart palpitations
Rubbery legs

141

Nausea
Trembling hands
My stomach turned to jelly
A ringing in my ears
Feeling like I'd drunk a litre of espresso
Temporary loss of hearing
Feeling like I was going to blackout
A conviction that I was going to die

I talked, he typed. I watched my words fill his computer screen.

'You're having panic attacks,' he concluded. 'This means your central nervous system is overloaded right now.'

He prescribed a drug – a beta blocker – called propranolol. He said it would slow my heart down and stop the attacks. He said other things too but he didn't tell me it was a highly addictive drug.

When I got home, I popped a pink pill out of a blister pack, washed it down with water and waited. An hour after I took it, the humming was mute again, my heartbeat slow and lazy. I lay on the floor, my cheek pressed against the carpet, the panic attacks already a thing of the past, my heart drunk on their absence. Years later, I would see the insanity of this. One drug for another. A passing of the chemical baton. Warm and familiar. All creases rolled out.

6

When he sighed, it was a sigh of pure want, need, joy. I knew that sigh. I'd ridden it all the way to hell.

'Ummm,' Dennis groaned.

He shook the ice cubes in his glass.

'Hear that?'

I heard it clearer than I heard my own heartbeat.

It was just after noon. I'd been out of hospital for a week.

'Gin and tonic,' he said. 'A delicious gin and tonic.'

I was already on his end of the phone, sipping his drink, him transported to my end of the phone, pale and sick, wanting that drink, that tornado of ice cubes, that sigh, like nothing on earth.

7

For two months, my stomach in tatters. The pain woke me early each morning. Gnaw. Gnaw. My digestive tracts could only handle the blandest of foods. Plain pieces of toast. Omelettes. Carrots. Mashed potato. Yoghurt. Soup. If I tried to eat anything fatty or greasy – like a strip of bacon – I'd get dizzy and nauseous and have to lie down, the room spinning the way it used to when I was drunk out of my mind. So thin. Bones jutting through my skin. When I tried to stop drinking in May, I weighed 13 stone 11 lbs. When I left hospital, I weighed dead on 11 stone. Reminds me of coming home after my first term at university, my weight down to 9 stone 10lbs. The shock on my parents' faces, my friends' faces, my doctor's face.

8

'Shall we fix a weekly appointment then? Every Saturday for an hour at ten am?'

Angie had the kind of eyes that stare straight through you and read all your secrets. When I called her, I was desperate.

'Although I'm a counsellor and psychotherapist,' she told me when we first spoke, 'my specialist field is hypnotherapy.'

She explained how hypnosis could be used to challenge and reconfigure deep rooted personality issues and traits. I liked the idea of having her turn me into someone else, so I arranged to see her for a trial consultation. What was £40 a session after all the thousands of pounds I'd spent on trying to escape myself? And how amazing if each £40 I spent changed a part of me.

'That sounds good,' I said. 'Every Saturday. Ten am.'

When she hypnotised me, it was magical. I didn't know much about hypnosis and I wasn't expecting it to be so powerful. It was like dreaming while awake. There was a mystical weightlessness too, like my body and soul were separated, floating in thin air, tingling, crackling with static, my ears buzzing, my throat numb and slack.

'We need to put you back together again,' she said, at the end of our first session. 'Build your confidence, your ego, your self awareness, your identity, your self-esteem. All of these things are non-existent.'

She 'got' me as quickly as Veronica. She was the safety net that broke my fall. She saved my life and then she changed it. She digested the story of my life, taking notes, nodding, shuffling the pieces of the jigsaw puzzle until they were ready to be fed back to me as streams of logic.

'That's not a good thing to get used to,' she said, when I told her about the propranolol. 'You need to learn to deal with life without any chemical helpers.'

'I feel so much better on them though.'

She was too sharp for my deviousness.

'Of course you do,' she said, outsmarting my attempt to outsmart her. 'Of course you do.'

9

When I went back to work, it was like walking into someone else's life. I didn't tell anyone – not even co-workers I was sort of friends with – what happened. I recycled the tired 'it was a stomach ulcer' speech until the lies made my eyeballs sting. People missed me, the 'me' who went missing. There were invitations to go to the pub at lunch time, after work, on Friday nights. I became an expert at making up excuses. I've got errands to run. I have to go to the post office. I'm meeting a friend. When I went out to lunch with clients – mostly work-hard, party-hard media buyers at ad agencies – I said I was taking antibiotics when they mocked me for ordering a bottle of mineral water. The days crawled by in a blizzard of paperwork and then it was dark again and I was in my car, driving home.

10

'If the craving is worst between five pm and seven pm then you need to create a distraction to break the pattern.'

Angie and I began each appointment by talking over the previous week's events, moods, emotions. She encouraged me to write in my journal as soon as I got into bed at the end of each day.

'Write about feelings. I want you to search deep inside yourself and pluck out only the most intense feelings. That's all that matters. The more you write, the more we'll have to work with.'

I found myself writing a lot about the habit of drinking, the routine, how I craved a drink every day at 5.30 pm like clockwork, how I was lost without the structure of addiction. We came up with a solution: dupe the craving by feeding it a 'drink'. I started drinking a hot mug of Ovaltine after dinner. No corkscrews, no glasses, no labels. Just simple things: the boiling of the kettle, the emptying of the sachet of Ovaltine into a mug, the pouring of the boiling water, the stirring of the drink with a little spoon, the smile as I took the first sip.

'What about something healthy? Like a herbal tea?'

I'd told Angie that the novelty of my daily Ovaltine had worn off. A few days later – after mentioning this at home – my parents bought me some Japanese green tea, a Japanese tea pot and some little cups.

'Great,' Angie said, at our next session, when I told her that the green tea lifted my spirits and put me in a good mood. 'This is the way forward. Keep working on yourself and new routines and habits will form. Ones that will change your life rather than destroy it.'

But then, as always, one pot of green tea stopped giving me the same kick, the same high, so I started to drink two pots a night instead and the high came back, playful and seductive.

11

It was freezing cold in the car park. I locked the car door and checked the lights were off. Now that I was sober, I noticed things like that. Small details surfaced in everything I did. I cared if I was shaving with a clean razor or if I had an umbrella with me on an overcast morning. Warm lights beckoned from inside the sports centre. I bought my ticket and hurried into the changing rooms. Other men of different ages and walks of life were busy drying off or getting into their swimming trunks. The anonymity was bliss. Nobody knew I was a recovering alcoholic. Nobody knew how out of control my life had been. Nobody knew I was trying to repair a body that had been depleted and annihilated by drinking. For a brief hour or two, I didn't feel ostracised from everything and everywhere. I'd leap into the pool, always hopeful that the icy water would shake some sense into me and swim lengths, counting one after the other after the other. After all those years of chaos, I wanted to put as much order into my new life as possible. After twenty lengths, the craving subsided and a calmness flooded my body. By the time I was back outside, crossing the car park, my breathing slower and more regular, what would earlier have been that all too familiar noise between my ears was now little more than a faraway whisper. My shoulders and arms would ache and I'd drive home along dark, deserted foggy back roads with the car stereo blasting.

12

When Laura found out from Mike that I'd been in hospital, she called and invited me to a party that she and her housemates were throwing.

'Why don't you bring your IV drip,' she said, mocking what I had just told her about my four days in hospital. 'It'll be the highlight of the party, watching you dance with it!'

Angie – homing in on Laura's negative influence as perceptively as Veronica before her – was frustrated with me.

'Why didn't you just hang up on her when she said this?'
Because no one calls any more.
'I don't know.'
I'm powerless when it comes to Laura.
'And are you going to this party?'
I can't remember the last time I went out at night.
'Yes.'

So, I decided to make my first nocturnal, sober, social venture out into the world at Laura's party. The deathwish was yet to be spring cleaned out of my bones . . .

I picked Mike up and we drove down to South London in the rain. Mike wasn't really in the mood to hear about my new-found sobriety. He got into the car with a bag of beer and popped a can before he even put his seatbelt on. I still remember how good that beer smelled.

'Hi,' she said, when we arrived, a cigarette in one hand and a bottle of beer in the other.

'God, you've lost so much weight.'

She was looking me up and down.

'Oh I know,' I replied. 'I used the I-almost-died-in-hospital diet. It's very effective.'

She laughed and ushered us in.

The party was smoky and crowded. The music was deafening. Everyone was drunk or stoned. So many red eyes. I tried to talk to Laura but we kept getting interrupted by her friends, the same people who kept offering me glasses of wine and joints and cigarettes. Laura came over to talk to me again. She was high and drunk. She took my hand and dragged me to her bedroom. She closed the door and locked it. The danger was turning us on. I leaned forward to kiss her. She drew back.

'That was awkward.'

'I'm sorry,' she said. 'It's just . . . a bad idea.'

She stank of beer and cigarettes.

'Why? I know you want me as much as I want you.'

'It's more complicated than that and you know it. I don't want to keep sleeping with you and then not talking for ages. It's too painful.'

Someone knocked on the door and called her name.

'I'm coming,' she yelled back.

She got up and left, without saying a word.

Later, when Mike and I were trying to leave, she came out of the kitchen, threw her arms around me and kissed me. I was angry with her but her lips were soft and her hips found my hands all too easily. Everything was familiar and then, just as the other people, the party, our history started to fade, she broke from me and pushed off into the party.

'Come on,' I said to Mike. 'Let's get out of here.'

'I want you to imagine yourself walking around a huge white house. Everything is white. The walls. The floors. The furniture. The curtains. This is a safe place, a peaceful place.'

There was no reality here. I was somewhere else. Angie's voice was far away. We spent a long time getting me this far into a trance state. Lots of deep breathing. Elements of the daily self-hypnosis exercises that Angie had taught me to do after I finished writing in my journal at bed-time.

'Now imagine yourself walking down a long white corridor. Look for a white door. Open it and enter the room. It's a big room. A bed. Curtains flowing in a relaxing breeze. Close the door behind you. Breathe nice and slowly. You feel a wonderful sense of relaxation. Nothing can hurt you. You are protected.'

There was silence for a while. A pause. I might have fallen asleep if I hadn't been aware that I was about to fall asleep. What's it like to get hypnotised? It's like watching your body sleep. It's being awake in your subconscious but asleep in your conscious. It's white light and the next world. Sleep without sleep. Being both here and there.

'Now,' she said, her voice close and hushed. 'I want you to press the middle finger and thumb on each hand together. Whenever you feel scared or uncomfortable or threatened in your everyday life, I want you to press your fingers and thumbs together and you'll remember the white house, the white room, the serenity, the amazing peace of mind.'

There was another lengthy pause. Pure happiness revolved around my head. I was suspended. Relaxed. Almost not breathing. My body had left me for a while. I was all soul, spirit.

'I'm going to count from one up to ten and then I want you to wake up in your own time.'

The numbers chimed inside my sleepy brain and then I opened my eyes and Angie was sitting on the black sofa opposite, smiling, welcoming me back to the world.

14

I paused at the end of the swimming pool. My lungs heaved as I tried to catch my breath. Fifty lengths. An hour in the water and I still felt like I was going to explode. I closed my eyes and let go of the pool-side. I dived down, down, down until I hit the bottom of the pool. I curled into a ball and held still. Everything was black. There was no noise. Trapped fifteen feet beneath water level I knew I was safe. There were no pubs or wine bars or cocktail bars or restaurants or off-licences or supermarkets or advertisements for Jack Daniels or inviting iced bottles of Budweiser or strangers thrusting drinks at me. My lungs swelled up. I pushed hard against the floor and rose upwards. I burst out of the water, gasping for air. I held the pool-side for maybe two or three seconds and then kicked off. Fifty-one, fifty-two, fifty-three, fifty-four, fifty-five . . . until I was too tired to feel anything.

15

I was the only sober person at the company Christmas party. I didn't throw any jugs of cream this time. I barely said a word all night. I must have been offered a hundred glasses of wine. There were a lot of empty toasts to things like 'a profitable new year'. Each time one of these toasts was made, I raised my glass of mineral water in the air as if it was a sign that read 'Sober And Uncomfortable'. After dinner, the party moved on to a club. There, as things got out of hand, someone threw a glass of beer over my head. I rushed to the toilets and tried to wash it off. It was in my hair, on my face, on my tie, down my shirt. The smell was incredible. Both repulsive and wonderful. I left straightaway, without saying a single goodbye. I drove home reeking of beer, craving beer, hating everyone. When I got in, I went straight to the bathroom, tore my shirt off and washed my hair. I kept scrubbing and shampooing, on and on and on, hoping to wash other things off too.

16

There was no snow that Christmas. There were no miracles either. I didn't wake up on Christmas Day suddenly able to drink again. My stomach started hurting again. I would learn in time, after seeing three different specialists, that this was psychosomatic. It hurt when I hurt. The craving was so bad. I didn't know what to do with myself. I took my pink pills. The Christmas tree was big and sad. The presents beneath it triggered a slew of childhood memories. Tying tinsel around my sister's head. She and I making brightly coloured paper chains. Decorating the tree. Hanging the lights. The turkey. The cranberry sauce. Our mother reading *Rudolph the Red Nosed Reindeer* to us at bed-time. The whole family gathered on Christmas Day. Everyone still young. The whole family gathered on Christmas Day.

17

I spent New Year's Eve 1994 watching Mike and Tina get drunk at a pub in London. They were still together. Every so often Mike shot a bourbon with his beer – something I 'taught' him to do. By the time they were slurring their words, they wanted me to dance with them. I squirmed as they tugged at my jacket. Sober, I was acutely self-conscious. I wasn't about to go out on any dance floor. When we were all sitting down again, their little splash of fun cut short, Mike told me I was being a killjoy. I didn't argue. My hands were empty. No cigarette, no glass. Minutes after midnight, I feigned exhaustion and left them in the pub, grinning like idiots. I drove home alone, fresh air blowing in through the windows, a New Year stretched out ahead of me like a frozen yawn.

18

Early in 1995, I went back to the hospital for a routine follow-up appointment. The specialist examined my stomach, checked my weight, measured my blood pressure, listened to my heart, sent me for blood tests. When the physical exam was done, she sat me down and asked me how I was.

'You were in quite a mess when you were admitted into hospital weren't you?'

I stared at my shoes. They needed a good polish.

'I know.'

I felt embarrassed. Maybe even a little judged.

'You seem to be doing much better.'

I figured that she was about thirty. I wondered if I'd still be 'doing much better' when I was thirty.

'Well, I've quit drinking.'

The words rushed out of my mouth.

'Good for you,' she said. 'I think that's really for the best. I don't think you could have carried on the way you were going.'

She gave me a nice smile. It said more than a hundred words ever could.

'Are you on any medication?'

I told her about the propranolol.

'Try not to stay on that for too long, it's bad for your body.'

I paid no attention. Quitting drinking was one thing, but quitting everything . . . I wasn't ready for that.

'Otherwise,' she said, getting up and opening the door. 'Keep up the good work with the no drinking.'

'Thank you,' I said and meant it.

19

'You have no idea how far you've come. When you first came to see me you couldn't hold eye contact, you were strung out beyond belief, your hands were shaky, you were as pale as a ghost and your conversation was littered with all the negatives – can't, don't, couldn't, wouldn't.'

Angie's house was warm as always. Some Saturdays, I wanted to stay there forever.

'I suppose so,' I said. 'But things just seem so dull. Nothing's changing fast enough. I feel like I'm banging my head against a brick wall. My job's boring. My social life is evaporating by the hour. Sometimes I wonder if it wouldn't have been easier to have just thrown my address book out of the car window on the way to hospital.'

She was so great when I got like that. She didn't rise to the bait of my bad moods. She just listened and sat there, reflecting back how despondent I was. Only when I was done, when everything was dripping down the walls of her lounge, did she cross the line and take me by the hand.

'It's going to take time. There are so many big things you need to do. Move out of your parents' home. Discover what it is you want to do with your life. Quit your job. Stop trying to medicate your moods. Find new friends. Break from Laura.'

She had a talent for reducing my chaos to a handful of concrete, clear sentences. Another time, she closed down a long, morbid, anxiety-stricken rant about the futility of life in the face of the inevitability of death by saying, 'Nick. You're not sixteen any more. This is something that bugs a sixteen-year-old, not someone who is twenty-four.'

20

Saturday nights were the worst. They just dragged and dragged. I knew that if I still drank then I'd have been out with the old gang: Dennis, Paul, Mike. Laughing, being stupid, having fun. Instead I was staying in with my parents or going to see films on my own, hiding in queues, sandwiched between couples and friends and families, praying that no one pulled the 'he's on his own' pity face. I just wanted the anonymity of a dark cinema. Once inside, I'd sink into a seat and lose myself in the film.

Sometimes, I'd spend a whole night driving around. Listening to music. Wheels spinning. Clocking up the miles. Trying to give myself the slip. I drove around London, sometimes around the old haunts, thinking of better days, worse days. Sometimes I drove past the pubs where Mike and I used to drink. Sometimes past the houses I went crazy in.

21

The Publisher burst out of his office with a magnum bottle of champagne.

'Everybody!' he shouted. 'Time to celebrate. We just floated the company on the stock market.'

His secretary stood smiling in front of several boxes of champagne flutes. When all fifty or so of us had flocked around him, he fixed his stare on me.

'Nick,' he called out. 'Could you open this bottle please?'

It was one of those make-or-break tests. Either I told him I didn't want to do it or I played it straight down the line.

'Of course,' I said and took the magnum from his hands.

I hadn't opened a bottle in five months. The cork hit the ceiling and then came the foam. I missed that excitable foam, we had once got along so well.

'Everybody. Take a glass,' barked the Publisher as he handed them out.

The ad manager who had turned super sleuth ever since I told him I'd been to see *When a Man Loves a Woman* waved his just-poured flute of champagne under my nose, hoping for further clues.

'Drink up Nick,' he said loud enough for everyone to hear, the glass butting against my chin.

'Get lost,' I said and shoved the glass away.

He was laughing. No one else was.

22

It was a long Sunday. I paced up and down my bedroom. The mirrors on the wardrobe at one end. Windows at the other. I sat down with a book. Read a few pages: couldn't relate to what I was reading. Threw the book down. Picked up my guitar. It was out of tune. I spent half an hour hunched over it, trying to get it in tune. The strings weren't interested. I gave up, put a record on. A song came blaring out of the speakers. A song I used to listen to before I went out drinking. I skipped to the next track. A sad song. Too sad. I decided to watch a video but I couldn't decide which one. I started skimming through my collection: *Frances*. *Taxi Driver*. *Bad Lieutenant*. *Betty Blue*. *Last Tango in Paris*. *Repulsion*. *Lilith*. *A Woman Under the Influence*. Forget it. I went over to the windows, stared through the glass. Birds hopped pathetically outside my bedroom window, their legs sometimes giving out on them as they looked for worms in the frosty grass. The window pane steamed up. I lay down on my bed. I wasn't tired. No hope of sleeping the day away. I thought of going out driving but there was nowhere I wanted to go. I decided that I didn't like the co-ordinates of my bed. I'd recently had a hunch that the bed was facing the wrong way. So I re-shuffled the furniture for the next two hours. Moved the bed here. The desk there. The chair here. The CDs there. I kept shuffling until everything clicked. It was eight times eight equals sixty four all over again. Now I was going to sleep facing in a new direction. This might work. A new lay-out. New co-ordinates. I could breathe again. The restlessness was gone. I sat down at my desk. A blank sheet of paper. A pen. A lot of unmanageable feelings. Words. So many words.

23

Our work was done. I knew it. Angie knew it. We were going around in circles. Six months sober. Stronger. Healthier. My doctor had taken me off all the stomach medication. Only the propranolol was left. I told Angie that it felt like phase one of my recovery was complete. She agreed. It was hard to stop seeing her but it was time. There was nothing more she could do for me.

24

After her party in December, Laura and I saw a lot of each other. We went out for dinner, for drinks, to see films. The mutual attraction, like the could-we-get-back-together topic, was off-limits. It wasn't that we weren't attracted to each other any more, it was just that sleeping together hurt too much. There was too much baggage. And so we gave up on getting back together and tried fooling ourselves into thinking that we could just be friends. But the love thing, the sex thing was always there, playing gooseberry. She drank whenever we went out but she never said anything when I didn't. I got into a habit of telling her about each hypnotherapy session and she would try and help me analyse what was going on. We got along better as friends. She was warmer as a friend. She let her guard down and was more intimate. I felt the same. We weren't wary of each other all the time. Things ticked along until she started seeing a new boy-friend – a throwback from university. After several nights out where I thought she was deliberately torturing me with endless details about her blooming love life, I wrecked everything. It was a Wednesday night in May. We were saying goodnight on Charing Cross Road. Out of nowhere, I told her I still loved her. I knew I'd made a mistake the second I said it. She flinched and rolled her eyes. Why can't we just be friends? she said. It's been so nice having you back in my life. Don't spoil things. She gave me a peck on the cheek and hurried off into the night. I stood with my hands in my pockets, wondering if her response would have been different if I still drank. We didn't call each other the next day, a routine we had fallen into over the past six months. Nor the day after. Or the day after that.

25

There couldn't have been more than twenty-five of us at most. We sat in rickety chairs around a marked table in a wooden hut that snuggled under the wing of an old church. The 12 Steps hung from the ceiling on a white banner. We sat sipping mugs of tea and coffee.

1 We admitted we were powerless over alcohol – that our lives had become unmanageable.

2 Came to believe that a Power greater than ourselves could restore us to sanity.

3 Made a decision to turn our will and lives over to the care of God *as we understand Him*.

4 Made a searching and fearless moral inventory.

5 Admitted to God, to ourselves, and to another human being the exact nature of our wrongs.

6 Were entirely ready to have God remove all these defects of character.

7 Humbly asked Him to remove our shortcomings.

8 Made a list of all persons we had harmed and became willing to make amends to them all.

9 Made direct amends to such people wherever possible.

10 Continued to take personal inventory and when we were wrong promptly admitted it.

11 Sought through prayer and meditation to improve our conscious contact with God as *we understood Him*, praying only for the knowledge of His will for us and the power to carry that out.

12 Having had a spiritual awakening as the result of these steps, we tried to carry this message to alcoholics, and to practise these principles in all our affairs.

Going to AA was like going to school. We were all there because we had to be there. We were getting educated too, just like we were children, teenagers, again, in the land of before – before being the first time we got drunk. The 12-Step Program was a kind of syllabus for those of us who thought life was only bearable if we had a glass of something sweet and strong in our hands. The meetings were classes, the 12 Steps the lesson, those of us there the dunces who had to go back and learn all the stuff we should have learned years ago.

My first AA meeting was a surprise, a revelation, a mystery. The 12 Steps were algebra to me. I saw the word 'God' and zoned out. I opened my mouth and found myself saying, My name is Nick and I'm an alcoholic. Almost immediately, I wondered if I agreed with what I had said. I had had only the vaguest of plans before I went to the meeting: to hide in a dark corner and keep my mouth shut. The decision to go had happened overnight. I was going out of my mind one Sunday afternoon when my parents suggested I call AA and go to a meeting. Two days later I was telling a room full of strangers that I was an alcoholic. I'd had no intention of making such a grandiose confession. It came as a shock. I spent the rest of the meeting trying to stifle a panic attack that was fighting to break through the smog of my propranolol dependence.

It was strange to be in a room with all those other people who had stopped drinking. We were a secret society, a private club. The entrance fee: sobriety. We had all chosen to be there. We all had one thing in common. We were all in varying moods. Not everybody would leave the meeting elated. Not everybody would leave the meeting with an empty heart. I left my first meeting feeling something in between. When a group prayer was recited *en masse* – 'God grant us the serenity to accept the things we cannot change, the courage to change the things we can, and the wisdom to know the difference' – I wanted to run for the door. When people in the meeting 'shared' their own experiences, I found myself identifying with a lot of what I heard. My mixed feelings about AA lay between those two things: the religious underpinnings of the 12-Step Program bothered me, the human interaction in the meetings was enormously moving. Beautiful even.

As I drove home that night, amazed that I'd admitted that I was an alcoholic, something seemed different. There was a lightness to the world. A summer breeze. A dog running wild. A plane in the sky. I thought of all the people that had come up to me after the meeting and introduced themselves and given me their phone numbers and said that I – a complete stranger – could call them at any time, day or night. Their compassion was overwhelming. I was almost scared off by such unconditional warmth.

When I got into bed, I dug around in my bedside drawers until I found it. That old book. The one I'd buried because it scared the hell out of me. *Alcoholism and the Facts*. The old library stamp on the inside of the jacket smiled at me, the scrawled 'Sale 50p' on the yellowing title page too. I propped myself up on two pillows and turned to the first page. God knows it was time.

26

'All alcoholics are extremely intelligent and extremely childish.'

It was August. Warm summer air gripped me by the throat. I was standing in another car park, after another AA meeting, talking with a kind, compassionate woman. Black hair, fifteen years sober. Smart, well dressed, funny, open.

She said her name was Barbara. She had cornered me

after the meeting and walked out into the car park with me. A few questions turned into an intense conversation.

And then that comment.

Like a baseball bat blow to the head. Boom.

She knew what she was talking about. Blackouts, cold sweats, vomiting, panic attacks, depressions, DTs, nightmares, broken promises, forgotten threats, bruises, fractures, cuts, scrapes with the law, death even.

'I was ashamed to even wake up in the end,' she told me.

She knew how I felt better than I did.

Some days it was like I didn't know anything. Right there, right then, all I knew was that I didn't want to drink again.

'There's nothing else to know,' she said, trying to make me feel better. 'Just knowing that you don't want to drink today is all you need to know.'

27

'What made you get in touch after all this time?'

The pub garden was noisy. Some teenagers were playing a drinking game.

'I just wanted to see you.'

Elizabeth sat opposite me, smoking a cigarette.

'Why though?'

To tell her why I really broke up with her. But I couldn't.

'I guess I wanted to show you how much I've changed.'

She exhaled. Out of the side of her mouth.

'So how long is it since you had a drink?'

'Almost ten months.'

'That's great. Do you feel better?'

'I think so. It's a mixed bag. Up and down, left and right.'

She smiled. We were both older now. She had been through her own stuff too. She told me stories that night that made me shiver. Drugs, cutting her arms and legs with knives, bulimia, her parents' divorce.

'You've always been like that, though, drinking or not drinking.'

'True.'

I had also got in touch with her because I wanted to hear her say something like that.

'Why don't you write?' she asked.

'I do.'

'I mean for a living.'

'Oh. I don't know.'

She pulled one of her faces. This one meant: you're downplaying yourself.

'Your poems used to make me cry.'

I shook the ice in the bottom of my Coca-Cola. Sober or not, I still couldn't take a compliment.

'You're probably biased,' I said. 'I shouldn't listen to you.'

We laughed.

It reminded me of all the other times we used to laugh.

Long ago.

Another lifetime.

28

'If you don't want to try again,' I said. 'Then say it. I'm sick of not knowing where I stand with you. This is it, once and for all. I'm going to walk out of that door in a second and you'll never see me again. If you don't want that to happen, then admit you still love me.'

Laura was drunk. We were in a pub in Clapham. It was the first time we'd seen each other since that night in May. I was going to call her, to clear the air – as part of my own ongoing experimental version of Step 9 – when she called me and suggested we meet up.

'Don't do this,' she said, curling her fingers around her glass.

'Just give me a Yes or No answer.'

She pulled a cigarette out of a crumpled pack and lit it.

'It's too dangerous,' she said with tears in her eyes. 'You really fucked me up. Of course I love you but you're too much. Nobody will ever be able to deal with you. You're too fucking intense.'

'At least I don't lie to myself and pretend I don't have feelings when I do.'

'Fuck you, Nick.'

'Where's your boyfriend tonight? Does he know you're seeing me? Or is this being presented to him as another of your classic two-boyfriend scenarios?'

I'd gone too far. She had tears in her eyes.

'I'm going to walk out of that door now unless you stop me.'

She stared into my eyes and said nothing. I knew it was time to give up Laura. I was addicted to her too. She had to go, just like the drink had to go. So I walked, her calling my name as I pushed one door open and closed another.

23 October 1995. One year sober. I kept saying it out loud. I was alone in my car heading to an AA meeting. When I got there, I was so happy that I got choked up as I sat at the back and listened to a young woman tell her moving story of alcoholism and recovery. At the end of the meeting, when we were all asked if there were any 'birthdays', I put up my hand. When my time to speak came round, I said that I was one year sober that very day. Everyone clapped. Barbara, who'd given me that life-changing talk in the car park, turned around from a few rows in front and smiled. She mouthed, 'I remember,' and the hairs on the back of my neck stood up. It was like a dream.

When I left the meeting that night, I sat in my car for a while, just watching the people file out of the church. Some stood huddled together in little groups, smoking and talking. Others hurried off to their husbands, wives, children, families, friends, empty homes, wrecked lives, long hours of loneliness. Winter was ripping everything to pieces but I didn't care. I started the engine and pulled away. The song on the car stereo was one I knew by heart. I started singing along, the applause at the meeting still ringing in my ears.

'You've got to do something,' my mother said. 'If you get any more depressed, you're going to be in trouble again.'

It was Christmas 1995. I was drowning. After my attempts to set things straight with Elizabeth and Laura, I hadn't heard from either of them again. Mike called once in a while but we never met up. Dennis was busy with a new girlfriend. Paul now lived and worked in Cardiff. There was no one left . . .

'I know,' I said. 'I just don't know what to do.'

I'd been going to a journalism course at night school since September.

'Leave your job. Move back to London. That's probably a good place to start.'

I knew I had to leave my parents' house. I was too old to still be living at home.

'I suppose I'll enrol on this sub-editing night school course. That lasts from January until March. Then I'll look for a new job and get my own place.'

My mother was nodding her head.

'OK. Do that.'

31

January 1996. Six o'clock. The Publisher called me into his office. He blamed me for the magazine's dwindling sales figures. I tried to defend myself. There was no passion though. I couldn't even pretend to give a shit. So he fired me. I left his office relieved. At least this was one thing that I didn't have to give up. It was just taken from me. How easy . . .

For every loss, a reward . . .

The reward was love. The woman I'd spent my whole life waiting for. The one who got me, the one who understood me. My Esther Greenwood. My blue beauty. Head of black curls. Petite and pale. My smiling twin. The part of me that had always been missing.

Anna had come to London to study for an MA. She and I had a mutual friend – Kristen, my old friend, maternal Kristen, whom I'd stayed in touch with ever since she went back to California – and when she left San Francisco, Kristen had given her my phone number. She rang me the day after I lost my job.

'Is that a good or a bad thing?' she asked when I told her.

'I hope it's a good thing,' I said. 'Anyway, what are you doing tomorrow night?'

'Nothing. What have you got in mind?'

'Let's go out for a drink.'

And we did.

All night, we talked until our throats hurt.

We didn't draw breath until they were putting the chairs on the tables and flicking the lights on and off in the bar, in a bid to get rid of us. I knew it was different. So different from anything I'd ever known before. I was so comfortable with her. I told her everything. Nothing sounded like a big deal. I said I was a recovering alcoholic and she just nodded. I told her about the depression, the panic attacks, hospital, hypnotherapy, losing all my friends, AA. She didn't flinch once. She understood, and by the time I dropped her back at her place, it was like we'd always known each other and were picking up from another time.

33

When it came to falling in love, there was no falling to do. Anna was as much of an outsider as I was. She was born in Paris to Polish–Jewish parents. When she was six, they emigrated to Los Angeles. When we met she'd come by way of New York and San Francisco. She'd travelled so far, had so many homes. I'd made my own journey too. The arcs of our journeys intersected. We collided. Just as we were meant to. There was laughter. So much of it. We shared the same references. Films. Books. Music. We taught each other to fly. To dream. Our love was a bubble that kept us safe. I never knew how unhappy I'd been until she showed what being happy really was. Everything seemed possible. Excitement was in the air. We had our own world. Two weeks after we met, we vowed to never be apart. I'd never pursued any woman like I pursued her. It was absolute. I'd never known love like this. Elizabeth. Laura. I loved them. But it wasn't the same. Anna loved the real me, the true me. And once I knew what that felt like, I knew I'd die without it.

34

It was April 1996. A warm spring evening. We'd run away to Paris together. Croissants for breakfast. Café mornings.

Afternoons spent walking along the banks of the Seine. Rodin. Picasso. Toulouse Lautrec. Shakespeare & Co bookstore. Père Lachaise Cemetery. Pink skies. Mass on Good Friday at Notre Dame. Mass on Easter Sunday at Saint Eustache. Henry Miller and Anaïs Nin. Sudden rainstorms. Lunch at Le Select. Montparnasse Cemetery. Jean Seberg's grave. Nights at repertory cinemas watching old John Cassavetes movies. Midnight on Pont Neuf. Red, yellow, blue lights across the water. Crème brûlée kisses. Unconditional love.

35

One night, after dinner, we wandered into Sacré-Coeur. I'd told Anna the story. Of sitting in those battered pews, praying for change. Hundreds of candles serenaded us. The air was thick with the volume of prayer. The choir sang their joyous hymns. Heads were bowed. Strangers wore their faith like armour. Our hands were joined together. It was like making love. I lit a candle and made a wish. We sat for a while. Happy to be happy. I led her to a quiet corner. I asked her to marry me. It seemed only right that I begin my new life where I'd made the decision to end my old life. She said yes. The mass was in full flow and the sweeping passages of soaring music might have knocked us off our feet had we not had each other to cling to. There were tears, only this time they were tears of love, not of shame and sadness. We left the cathedral, the whole of Paris spread out before us, and sat down on the steps, just holding on to each other, not saying a word, thinking how lucky we were to have found each other.

In June, we flew out to Los Angeles to see Anna's parents. Midway through our stay, we took off on a road trip to visit Raymond Carver's grave in Port Angeles, a small town in Washington. His writing had haunted me ever since I discovered him when I was eighteen. During my first year sober, the story of his life – moving from alcoholism and despair to sobriety and love – gave me hope, and now I wanted to thank him. We left Seattle around noon and drove north through the forests. By the time we found the cemetery, it was raining hard and getting dark. It was set in a clearing in a forest at the end of a dirt track. The edge of the cemetery curled off a cliff face into the Pacific Ocean. We had to use Anna's cigarette lighter to find his grave because it was so dark. One of the poems that Carver wrote as he was dying from cancer, 'Gravy', was etched in the stone. It was a poem that I'd read a hundred times when I drank and never connected with. Now, with Anna by my side, sober, it put a lump in my throat. *No other word will do. For that's what it was. Gravy./ Gravy, these past ten years./ Alive, sober, working, loving and/Being loved by a good woman. Eleven years/ago he was told he had six months to live/at the rate he was going. And he was going/nowhere but down. So he changed his ways/somehow. He quit drinking! And the rest?/After that it was all gravy, every minute/of it . . .* Anna and I stood hugging each other, in the dark, in the middle of nowhere, soaked to the bone, crows squawking all around us, the ocean roaring, the trees whistling, the wind chimes tied to Carver's grave singing their eerie song, and then we hurried back to the car, eager to get back to life, the open roads, journeys in progress.

'This is getting ridiculous.'

I was busy chopping a propranolol pill into thirds.

'What now? Thirds? Quarters? Fifths? Sixths?'

It was really hard to get equal thirds because the pill tended to split under the pressure of the blade.

'I'm doing more thirds,' I said.

'And then what?' Anna asked. 'You're going to try snorting halves for breakfast? I mean, come on. It's a joke. Why don't you just get off them?'

I'd started playing with the dose on the advice of my new doctor. I'd gone to see him because the propranolol was wiping me out. I was working nights for a tele-sales company close to our flat in Camden and writing about music for *Melody Maker* the rest of the time. He suggested that I start chopping the pills into whatever dose I thought I needed.

'I'm trying to. It's difficult.'

After seeing the doctor I tried taking a quarter of a pill a day. At first, I got my energy back. I was in good spirits. I felt great. Then I couldn't sleep. After a massive panic attack swooped down on me while Anna and I were in a supermarket checkout queue, I went back to taking a whole pill a day. Now, I was playing pharmacist again.

'But that's real life. Panic attacks happen. You can't avoid them.'

Perfect thirds whispered 'She's wrong' from the chopping board.

'I know,' I said and swallowed a third of a pill.

'Happy Two Years Sober.'

Anna gave me a kiss. We were having a romantic dinner. No AA this year. I'd stopped going. Something had kept me from those meetings. I kept telling myself I was bothered by the God stuff and by the idea of devoting so much time to talking about how I didn't drink any more. Honestly, though, I was still in denial. My brain was dulled with propranolol and going to meetings made my skin crawl. It was too painful, too raw. And I knew that taking medication was frowned upon by AA. I got angry the first time someone lectured me about how I shouldn't take any medication – like beta blockers, antidepressants, tranquillisers – because it sets up more addictive patterns. As far as I was concerned, propranolol had played a big role in making my sobriety possible. In truth, though, I was angry he and all the others after him were right.

'Thank you.'

She poured me a glass of sparkling mineral water.

'I'm proud of you,' she said and we raised our glasses for a toast.

39

Everything was perfect on paper. I was more than two years sober, busy writing my first book, working for *Melody Maker*; I'd quit my tele-sales job, Anna had a good job. There was something wrong though. My moods were erratic because of the irregular propranolol doses.

Some days, I took two pills, others I took a quarter at night only. I was run down and kept getting minor bugs and infections that winter: colds, sore throats, blocked sinuses, the flu, viruses. Then, as I started to worry about what was wrong with me – as usual convincing myself that I had countless illnesses – my stomach started to hurt again. Sharp pain. Nausea. Days when I couldn't eat. Meals of boiled cabbage and soup. It was like the bill for all the abuse had finally arrived. And I did nothing about it. No AA. No therapy. No writing in my journal. No self-hypnosis exercises at bed-time. Not even any swimming or cycling any more. I just festered, all the way through to late summer 1997.

40

'You've been taking propranolol for almost three years. I think it's time we weaned you off it.'

September 1997. A new flat on the border of King's Cross and Bloomsbury, another new doctor.

'But every time I try and come off it, I get panic attacks and feel strung out and then I can't sleep.'

She chewed her lower lip, deep in thought.

'We'll do it slowly, starting with a lower dose from tonight. And I'll refer you to our counsellor. This way, you'll get some solid support as you make a clean break from it.'

It sounded like the last thing I wanted to do. I took the new prescription from her like it was a curse.

41

My sleeping patterns went haywire. I woke up early in the morning and couldn't get back to sleep. I went to bed late and couldn't get to sleep. I was grinding my teeth at night, loudly enough to wake Anna up. Some nights, she woke to find me sleep-walking. The panic attacks came by the swarm. On the tube. On the bus. In the bath. While I was waiting for the kettle to boil. The craving for a drink came back. Gnashing, bright fangs. I was unravelling. It felt like it was October 1994 all over again and I'd only just stopped drinking.

42

'Would you like some healing?' the counsellor asked.

'Healing?'

I didn't know what she meant. But I was ready to try anything.

'Reiki healing.'

'OK,' I said.

She got up.

'Can you lie on the bed please?'

I got on to the bed.

'You can close your eyes or leave them open,' she said, her soft voice reminding me of Angie.

I closed my eyes.

'What are you going to do?'

'It's a simple process of "laying on of hands". I will lay my hands just above your body and free your energy blockages and obstructions. I'm going to re-direct your energy flow and correct it.'

My heart was thumping.

'Breathe nice and slowly,' she said, her voice now a faraway whisper.

I concentrated on my breathing. Angie's voice came into my head, warm and comforting. *You feel as though you're weightless. You haven't a care in the world. You're bathed in a pure, white light. It protects you.* My lungs slowed up, my heart slowed up, the anxious tremor in my hands settled down.

'How do you feel?' she asked in a lighter-than-air whisper.

It was our second appointment. I'd felt so weird after the first session – disoriented, exhausted, anxious, dizzy – that I almost didn't go back.

'Nauseous and like I'm floating. My legs and arms feel numb.'

'OK, just let yourself go.'

The bed floated beneath me. I could sense her hands as they hovered inches above my body.

'I feel scared now,' I said. 'It's as if I'm rising into the air.'

'There's nothing to worry about.'

Random images were spilling into my conscious, a memory rainstorm, bits and pieces of my past blowing everywhere. An image of my dead grandfather came to me and then drifted away.

'I just saw my dead grandfather,' I mumbled.

She laughed.

Why was she laughing?

'Don't be afraid,' she said. 'Sometimes spirits contact people while they're being healed. It's quite common.'

'Spirits?'

I opened my eyes, desperate to return to the real world. She was still standing there in her blue blouse and grey skirt. She was smiling at me when my eyes re-adjusted to the bright lights.

'Now, we need to wash our hands like we did last time,' she said walking over to the sink in the corner.

'Why do we need to wash our hands?' I'd asked her when she did this after our first session.

'To cleanse the energies,' she'd explained.

I put my hands under the cold water like we did at the first session and then dried them on the paper towel she handed me.

'Are you feeling all right?' she asked.

'I feel like I did last week. Really dizzy, like my legs have turned to rubber.'

'That's normal. When you get home, drink lots of water and make sure you rest.'

She opened the pine wood door and ushered me back out into the medical centre waiting room.

43

The healing was too much in the end. There were nightmares afterwards, panic attacks. She wasn't helping me, she was making things worse. Anna and I decided that I shouldn't go to the remaining sessions. Instead, I would find a private therapist. Her name was Diane. The first session was OK, mostly background information. The second one, a brief dip into the murkier stuff, the secrets.

'I used to cut myself.'

She flinched, sat back in her chair.

'Why did you do that?' she asked, her jaw frozen wide open.

'It helped me cope.'

The look of disgust on her face said everything I needed to know.

'It never hurt when I was doing it,' I said, getting defensive. 'It was a way to blank out the other pain, the stuff that's invisible.'

If there's one thing I've learned from all this, it's to walk away when you know someone's never going to get 'it'. After that session, I never went back.

44

'Hi, my name is Nick and I'm an alcoholic.'

'Hi Nick,' came back a chant of fifty or so voices.

The room was musty. It was a cold Wednesday night in November. I struggled to find the words I was looking for. They were unformed as yet, shapeless, hesitant. I could hear feet nervously shuffling under the wooden tables. Somebody coughed. A woman opposite me was clinging to a Styrofoam coffee cup. Steam was rising out of it. The woman who was running the meeting smiled at me. Sound emerged from the back of my throat, 'I have a story to tell.'

45

AA was different this time around. I went to meetings with an open heart and found what I needed. Trust. Comfort. Support. Warmth. Compassion. There was regret too.

Regret that I hadn't gone back sooner, that I'd not worked through the 12-Step Program with a sponsor, that I hadn't played by the rules. If anyone thinking of quitting drinking asked me if they should go straight to AA or not, I would say, Go, before it's too late. I spoke a lot at these meetings. I wanted to voice hope, share hope. There were people there who'd just quit. People at the beginning of the slide. People fresh out of hospital. I remembered what those early weeks and months were like. So much fighting with yourself, with the world. I was surprised by how much I wanted to help everyone in those meetings. Their lives, their problems seemed easier to decipher, much easier than my own. I was in a fog. I went back to AA because something was crumbling inside me.

46

No cure cured me. I was bouncing from one feelgood remedy to another, patching my sobriety up just as I had patched my drinking life up with a string of short-term solutions. Soon, one AA meeting wasn't enough. I found myself flicking through the London meetings directory at all times of the day and night. I was also spending a lot of time on Recovery Link, a twenty-four hours a day, seven days a week, on-line chat group for recovering alcoholics and drug addicts. It became disabling, dangerous. I started to feel as though I couldn't do anything myself. My independence, my stubbornness, the things I valued about myself, were drifting away. I was becoming a child again, in constant need of approval, support. I stopped believing in myself, that all the strength I needed to stay sober, to keep moving ahead, was inside, and started to believe that it was all outside. If I woke up in a bad mood, I ignored my work and looked for help on Recovery Link. If I craved a drink, I didn't sit it out and wait for it to pass, I ran to AA. So one day I threw the meetings directory in the bin and resolved to go it alone. No more meetings. No more Recovery Link. It's my life, my mess. They're my problems. It's my responsibility.

47

But of course that didn't mean me facing up to my problems. I wasn't ready for that. I just wanted to keep hunting for the cure. I prowled health food stores like they were off-licences. I took handfuls of vitamins with breakfast each morning. I tried every kind of herbal tea I could find. I couldn't stop searching. It was a heartbreaking obsession. I refused to give up and accept the things I couldn't change. I'm not a quitter. Never have been. Never will be. The patch-ups came thick and fast and all of them worked for a few days, sometimes weeks if I was lucky, and then failed me: Sleepytime Tea, St John's Wort, ginseng, ginkgo biloba, kava kava, lavender oil, Quiet Life herbal tablets, Kalms, camomile tea, feng shui . . .

48

Florence. Such a beautiful city. Anna and I had gone away on a last-minute holiday. I was restless, unable to focus.

'Why don't we drive to Monte Carlo?' I said over breakfast one morning.

'Have you lost your mind?'

We had a map out on the table. We had talked about driving to Pisa but that was an hour or so from where we were staying.

'We've never been there. Why don't we go?'

'We're in the middle of Italy. It's eight am. Monte Carlo is all the way over there.'

She followed the map with her finger.

'So what?' I said.

And that was that. We got in the rental car and I drove. Nine hours later we were in Monte Carlo. It was early evening. We had two of the most expensive drinks we'd ever bought, walked about for an hour, watched people suffocate on their diamonds and pearls and then got back in the car.

'I'm falling asleep,' Anna said.

We were going in and out of tunnels, clinging to mountain roads.

'It's OK,' I said. 'I'll wake you when we get there.'

We didn't get back until dawn was breaking. Even then, I still wasn't tired. I wanted to keep driving. To Milan. To Madrid. To Berlin. To Budapest. I wanted to go somewhere and leave myself behind. But wherever I went, I got there first.

49

I'd lost any notion of what 'normal' is. I was living a 'normal' life. I just didn't know it. I panicked if I got too stressed about something or if work was getting me down.

I had unrealistic expectations of what life could be. I thought that just because I quit drinking, I should be happy all the time. I thought that just because I quit drinking, then I could never get depressed again. I'd spent so much of my life medicating my moods that I no longer knew what a 'normal' mood was.

50

I got so strung out I thought I would explode into a thousand tiny pieces. There was a solution though, one I'd been thinking about a lot: I hadn't thrown away my unused supply of propranolol as the doctor had asked me to do. Instead, I'd buried those pills in the medicine cabinet – just in case. And when the 'just in case' became reality, I unscrewed the cap and peeped in at those pink pills, those thought-mufflers. I remember shaking and wondering if I was about to destroy everything. I had to have something. I'd bailed on AA. I'd bailed on healing. I'd bailed on therapy. I was prescribing assorted herbal remedies in the hope that some mix of something would peel me off the ceiling. I shook a pill into the palm of my hand. I put it on my tongue and washed it down with some water. There. Gone. Done. I didn't care. I closed my eyes and walked in slow motion into a shower of beautiful fireworks.

51

Two weeks of random propranolol-popping later, I went cold turkey again. The bliss of not having to think clearly, of waving goodbye to the panic attacks, of feeling like I could breathe again, soured as the initial ecstasy gave way to the dull grind of addiction, routine. Side effects stuck pins in my flesh. The dose was either too strong or not strong enough. When they stopped working, I put the bottle back in the medicine cupboard and told Anna that whatever happened, no matter how desperate I got, she wasn't to let me fall back on those pills again. So why didn't I flush the rest of the pills down the toilet? Such cunning . . .

52

'Everything in your body is red, hot, angry. You are blocked with internal heat: anxiety, anger, depression, frustration, stress, panic, restless sleep, stomach problems, headaches. All of these things are caused by internal heat. I need to give you some herbs which will relax you and release the heat.'

Attempt to fill the void #6 million. This time: Chinese medicine. Same origin as all the other would-be cures. I read a newspaper article. I saw something on TV. Somebody told me something about it. You can pretty much fill in the blanks. The withdrawal from propranolol was bad. Panic attacks, insomnia, rage, no concentration, edginess, uncontrollable energy levels, morbid anxiety, stomach pain, depression. So I went to see this Chinese doctor and asked him if he could give me something to help me relax. He examined my tongue and took my pulse and asked me questions about my diet and lifestyle habits and then he made his diagnosis. I was sent home with seven large plastic bags filled with what looked like twigs, tree bark and random foliage from a forest. I had to boil a bag of herbs for thirty minutes every evening and then drink a single cup of the result: a dark brown liquid that tasted like soil. An hour after I drank the first cup of this potion, my muscles popped and a syrupy relaxation calmed my body and mind. Aaah, that feels better. It was the first time I'd felt like myself in weeks.

This latest miracle cure – and of course I told everyone I knew, as always, that I'd finally found the thing that put me in balance – soured too. When I finished the fortnight's prescription of herbs, the panic attacks and the constant anxiety came straight back. Silvery and ruthless. I kept waking up at 4 or 5am and not being able to get back to sleep. I'd lie in the dark, going out of my mind. Thinking the same thoughts. That the headaches plaguing me must be a brain tumour. That the stomach pain was now an early warning sign of stomach cancer. That my insomnia meant I was having a nervous breakdown. When I exploded at the dinner table one night and threw an Evian bottle across the room and shouted and yelled about how much I wanted, needed, had to have a drink, the look of horror on Anna's face told me I had hit a wall in my sobriety.

53

So I started drinking again. Coffee, that is. I had to fill the black hole inside with something: a vice. To most people, the idea of drinking coffee or not drinking coffee means nothing in the scheme of things. Coffee was just another vice that had to go when I came out of hospital. Now, almost four years later, I drank a cup of thick, dark French coffee and felt like I was close to falling off the wagon. Today, coffee. Tomorrow, cigarettes. The day after, a glass of wine. It doesn't work like that but I thought it did and after having that cup of coffee – which made me so happy – I swore off it for a full week before I enjoyed another cup. But I realised I couldn't bleach all pleasure out of my everyday life. I needed something. Soon, I was enjoying all kinds of coffee: espresso, cappuccino, filter, instant. It was heaven. Then I decided to take up smoking cigars. At first, just a big fat one on a Saturday night, and then, little cigars on weekday nights, and then, a little cigar after breakfast. And then, how many left? What if I run out? Do I have enough money to buy an extra pack just in case? Then, a pack a day. Then, ten, fifteen cigars a day. And then: no more. The end. Nicotine jitters. Foul temper. Insomnia. Tremors. Hunger. Fury for being so weak. For slipping. Propranolol. Coffee. Cigars. Finally: nothing but a brain that wouldn't stop jumping up and down, pleading for some sweets to munch on.

54

Did I miss drinking? Really, truly miss drinking? It was starting to feel like I did. Did I miss the self-medication? The order? The drinks themselves? The ritual? The security of drowning in a bottle of wine each night? I kept reminding myself of the other things: the vomiting blood, the hangovers, the DTs, the people I hurt, the crying, the broken health, the blackouts, hospital. It still didn't make any sense. How could I miss something that had made me so unhappy? How could I even be considering it? But I was and the pull to my old life was strong and wore me out.

55

It amazes me how strong Anna was through all of this. She anchored me, held steady, as I rushed from here to there like a maniac. I exhausted her with my limitless energy and my need to analyse everything in minuscule detail. She was always patient and understanding. Often, she'd come home from work to find a bottle of wine already uncorked on the table.

'Why is that open?' she'd ask.

'I'm letting it breathe.'

'Oh,' she'd say, her tone of voice understandably wary.

Of course, I did want her to enjoy the wine. I'd learned all the tips over the years. But, really, I was playing Russian Roulette. I'd buy wine for dinner, uncork it early in the afternoon and then tease myself. I'd raise the bottle to my nose and breathe in, eyes closed, dreaming, dreaming, dreaming. I was testing myself, daring myself. But I was too strong for that. I'd wait until my throat and mouth and stomach were watering, screaming for that wine and then I'd put it down on the table and go back to my desk and do some work. One night, I told Anna why I was really uncorking the bottles before she came home.

'I knew you were testing yourself', she said.

'How did you know?'

'Come on,' she said. 'How well do I know you? The only reason I didn't say anything or tell you to stop torturing yourself, was because I knew you'd never actually do it. And besides, this whole "Can I drink again" dilemma is something that you and only you are going to figure out.'

56

Anna and I set a date to get married. Saturday 24 April 1999. Every day from then until the wedding: the same picture in my head. Here comes the bride. Sipping champagne. Here comes the groom. Sipping champagne. Cut. No. Re-shoot the scene. Here comes the bride. Sipping champagne. Here comes the groom. Sipping mineral water.

57

Two, three nights a week, I went out running. I was trying to burn off energy. I was trying to break the pattern that had me working every day, every night, taking on more and more projects in a bid to wallpaper over the war going on inside me. I'd get home, soaked with sweat and take a shower. For an hour, I'd be relaxed, high on endorphins, and then it would all start up again. The machinery of my distress. Noise. Heat. Steam. Crunch. Grind.

58

So many times, Anna and I had talked about cutting, about self-harm, self-injury, self-inflicted violence, whatever you want to call it. When I first told her about it, weeks into our relationship, she was compassionate and curious where others had been shocked and disgusted. Whenever I tried to explain why I cut myself, I tended to fall back on the same explanations: that it was a coping mechanism, a way to take emotional pain and make it physical, a way to feel something when I had shut down, a way to release unbearable feelings, a language stronger than words. The scars, the legacy of those desperate times, had mostly faded and only the ones from that near-fatal acid trip remained. Sometimes they're more prominent, other times not. But the history is always there. I decided that I wanted to try and make my peace with it so I bought two books about self-harm/injury – Steven Levenkron's *Cutting* and Tracy Alderman's *The Scarred Soul* – and Anna and I immersed ourselves in researching the topic and trying to figure out why: why I did it. Why I needed it. Why I stopped.

59

It was our Wedding Day. Anna and I walked down the steps of the registry office through a shower of confetti. We posed for some photographs and then got into the white stretch limo that had been hired to take first us, and then other guests, to the reception. A cluster of hands waved from the other side of the mirrored windows. As the wheels started to roll under us, Anna lowered the electric windows.

The sun had come out. I reached forward and pulled a bottle of champagne out of one of several iceboxes that littered the car. I tore the gold foil off the bottle's cap and unwound the wire casing. I told Anna to grab a glass from the cabinet on the limo wall. My heart was thumping. There was frenzy in my fingers as I popped the cork. The champagne flooded out of the bottle and, as it always used to, reminded me of violent waves breaking up on a sea shore. Sea foam, champagne foam, all of it so damn romantic.

We were crawling past thousands of people on the street. Past, present and future was now replaced by something more immediate and more detached. I was so happy that I forgot everything. Forgot I was a recovering alcoholic. I could smell the champagne in the air. I could taste it on my dry lips. I could hear its tiny bubbles breaking and shattering like crystal falling on a stone floor. Life was flowing through me. What does it matter? It all happened so fast. I was perched on the edge of the black leather seat. The driver turned some music on. It was thumping out of the speakers from all directions. Anna took a sip from her champagne glass. I had never sipped champagne.

Anna says that I got a 'crazy look' in my eyes. I was caught up in the romance of it all. I wanted the champagne, the loving eyes, the sunshine, the band of gold on my finger, everything. Someone at an AA meeting once told me that alcoholics don't live, they need. I told Anna that I was going to have a glass of champagne. I leaned over and scooped up a second glass. A great looking glass. Refined stem, pretty shape.

For a moment in the back of that limo, time stood still. I was going to have that drink. A spring snapped inside me. I wanted to cut myself free. I wanted to be normal, just for a day. I wanted a genie to leap from the bottle and grant me one wish. An impossible wish. That I could drink for just one day and have it not count . . .

I went to pour out the champagne, trembling at the thought of downing it in one shot, of the bubbles burning up my nose, of the champagne scorching my throat and oesophagus and then that wonderful calm like a rusty old anchor being dropped into the ocean in slow motion. Aaaaaah. The window-shaking sigh. The flutter in the stomach and then peace: hands, even outstretched, as steady as a rock; heartbeat slow and regular, thoughts fluid and linear; a warm glow of self-confidence and safety blazing in my soul; a life travelling at a thousand miles an hour slowing to a hundred miles an hour, wind blowing through my hair, the passing landscape visible rather than a blur.

Anna took the glass away from me and then the bottle. I was dazed. I didn't know what was happening. Here, she said, drink this. She handed me a can of Tango. I tore back the ring-pull and started drinking it. The car hit some dense traffic. I could hardly breathe. I was suffocating. Then I felt her hand take mine. It's OK, she said. It's a big day. It's a very big day.

The next day, when we were flying at 30,000 feet on our way to Rome, Anna turned to me and told me that it was the closest that she had ever seen me come to relapsing. I didn't say anything but it gave me the chills.

60

When we got back from our honeymoon, we went back to living in our bubble. People kept asking us if we felt different now that we were married. We didn't. We were just glad to be alone again. The wedding was for everyone around us. A chance for them to step inside the bubble for one day. As soon as we had our space back, I sat down one night and wrote about that near slip in the back of the limo. I just wanted to get it off my chest, to put it somewhere. What I thought was going to be a night's writing became this book. I couldn't stop. I went into overdrive. I wanted to tackle my past, to make sense of it, to put it into order.

61

Five months later. September, tight like a scarf. Bonfire smoke. Memories of shuffling through heaps of leaves on school breaks. My parents sleeping. My sister on the phone in her bedroom talking to her boyfriend. Me: back in my old bedroom. Now a spare bedroom. But to me always my bedroom, even in a hundred years' time, when I'm dead and someone else sleeps in it.

The room was full of memories: vomiting up the walls in my sleep, Elizabeth, cutting myself, the skull crushing depressions, Laura, getting drunk listening to music on headphones, bottles of bourbon, the jobs, hospital, recovery, getting fired, the friends I used to have. Ghosts danced around my bed. Far away, so close. I tried to concentrate on the Anne Sexton biography I was reading. I wasn't interested in anything but Anne Sexton. Her battle with depression and alcoholism. Her suicide. Her bruised vocabulary. I was in a time warp. I was seventeen again. Except I wasn't reading *The Bell Jar*. I was reading Anne Sexton's poetry. I should have realised that I was back to the beginning of the slide. That depression was driving its nails through my hands and feet again.

*   *   *

Anna was away in Amsterdam on a work trip. I was staying with my family. I didn't tell them but I was too frightened to be alone. My moods were terrifying. I was scared that I might do something stupid. When I turned up at their house, my mother said I was too thin, that I needed feeding up. We'd been through that scene so many times before. She said I was 'worked up' and 'incredibly anxious'. Anna rang me every night. Each time she called, my mind was more scrambled. I spent most of our phone calls up in my old bedroom, sobbing.

'Why are you crying?' she asked the first time she rang.

'Because I feel like I'm dying inside.'

Later, when everyone was asleep and the house was quiet, I saw flashes of the truth. That my optimism was a flat tyre, that my strength of will was a black eye. I was falling to pieces. And then, I lay very still in bed, reading about another of Sexton's suicide attempts, tears crawling down my cheeks.

62

That autumn came with a scowl. It was like all the colour had been bleached out of the streets. Brown buildings. Grey buildings. I wasn't sleeping or eating properly. Every night, I went to bed early because I was so tired, but as soon as my head hit the pillow, I was wide awake again. It was a cruel joke. When I could get to sleep – at 2 or 3am – it was never for long. I'd wake again sometime around 5am. The worse my sleep got, the more I obsessed about it. Soon I was lying in bed unable to sleep because I'd spent the whole day wondering if I'd be able to get to sleep that night. The snowball grew a little bigger each day. One night, I lay in bed, and asked myself, Am I awake or am I asleep and dreaming that I'm awake? I had no idea. I wasted the rest of the night arguing with myself about which was the right answer. By the time I was sure that I was awake, the birds were chirping and another day was dragging me to life. I got out of bed and it started up again: am I dreaming that I'm cleaning my teeth or am I really cleaning my teeth?

All throughout summer, bulbs had been blowing out in my head. There was nowhere left to hide. I was so tired all the time. When I went running, mostly at night or early in the morning, it took enormous effort for me to talk myself into putting my trainers on and going out. Why bother? What good will a stupid run do me now? Shall I go? I'd ask Anna. Yes, she'd say. You need to. I'd finish tying my laces and head out. People would rush past me and I'd want to stop and ask them how they kept going, how they didn't let death wreck their lives. There was so much death in my head. Funerals. Elegies. Cemeteries. Orchids. My brain was short-circuiting on morbid images. Some days, embalmers and undertakers were all I thought about. And when I say that, I don't mean to suggest that I had any control over what I was thinking. These thoughts were vermin from the part of my brain that had become a No Go zone. It was burned out. Dangerous. Loose cables. Live wires sticking from the walls like antennae. Rubble. Flooding. Only a fool would have tried to go in there.

Once I stopped sleeping, the cracks turned up in just about every other area of my life. Food was an irritation, something to be pushed around plates that I didn't want to dirty because it would only create more washing up to do. Washing up, like cooking, like taking a bath, like shopping, became an ordeal that I could barely face going through with. Vacuuming the lounge left me exhausted and breathless. Washing my hair made my arms ache. Shaving left me shaking.

This gentle undoing of my life was like watching a thread come loose. I started to lose weight. Trousers that were usually a little too tight began to hang about my hips. My working life became a war. I wasted entire days staring at my computer screen. All I did was make cup after cup of coffee – most of which I forgot about as soon as I had made them. Hours later, I would take a sip from one of these many cups and realise that it had long since gone cold.

There were days when I would start crying for no reason. Everything was so crisp, so real. I was standing still, eyes closed, as this depression rolled over me. I was too tired to try and escape any more. So I stopped. I just stood there and let it catch up to me. And when it did, it struck like a tidal wave. There was this weight against the back of my head. Too great to describe. Giant puppet hands slapping my skull all day, every day. Without alcohol or drugs or any kind of escape, I had nothing to defend myself with. The blizzard blew through me for weeks. It got so cold. I longed for a bottle of vodka. Anything to obliterate the drone in my head. To silence. Numb. If only for a night. There was nowhere to go. Nowhere to hide. When I broke down crying, I couldn't explain why. One night, when I was crying in the kitchen, Anna kept asking me why I was so upset. The best answer I could come up with was: 'I've gone missing.'

'What's that supposed to mean?'

'It's just how I feel,' I said. 'I can't put it any other way. I can't find myself.'

Anna tried everything. Buying me books she thought I'd get excited about. Booking tickets to see an old film she knew I loved. Getting me to help her cook an elaborate dinner. When none of these things brought me back to life, she panicked.

'I think you need to get into therapy,' she said one night. 'You're getting worse every day.'

'It's OK. It's just a rocky patch.'

'But you've been fighting this for so long now,' she said. 'When are you just going to stop and face yourself?'

The pasta on my plate looked overwhelming. Like an aerial view of an entire country. Anna had already finished hers, the remnants of the tomato sauce leaving curls and swirls all over the white expanse of her empty plate.

'I'm not going to give up. That's not what I'm about. I will not resign myself to this shitty mood and just lie down and let it rip me to pieces.'

'But it's already tearing you to pieces.'

A sad song was playing softly in the background. I can't remember what it was. I've tried. But I can't.

'Maybe,' I said. 'But what have I always said? I got depressed because I drank. Part of the deal was that if I gave up drinking, then I'd never get depressed again.'

'I think you've got it back to front,' she corrected. 'I think you drank because you were depressed.'

I thought the windows were going to blow out.

I had shut down a long time ago. Maybe as long ago as when the doctor took me off propranolol. I lost a little ground every week. I tried to stall its progress, its assault. I put up a fight. And by the time it had overrun me, I was in deep denial. I'm fine. I'm OK. I'll be better next week. Small things picked me up: a film, a dinner, Anna's smile, work, a relaxing bath, a day off, a night when I could sleep. And these things made me feel that I had been making it all up. That it was all in my mind. That I wasn't depressed. It was just a down period. It was working too hard. It was not going out enough. It was working from home. There are always a million excuses. But Anna knew. She saw through my see-saw moods. The days when I hardly spoke followed by days when I planned trips to Italy or dragged her off on shopping sprees. She let things coast for a while and then, when she knew I was slipping away, she rang the alarm bell.

'Please see a therapist.'

She was desperate. Tears in those beautiful blue pools for eyes.

'I will.'

'You keep saying you will but you won't call anyone.'

'I'll do it soon.'

'Look at you,' she said. 'You're wasting away. You're not eating. You're not sleeping. You don't want to go out. You don't want to do anything. You don't want to see anyone. You're obsessed with your health. I don't know what to do any more.'

There were so many aches and pains in my body. I thought I had so many different illnesses. Anna couldn't talk any sense into me. Every day, I regaled her with my latest symptoms and diagnoses.

'But what if I am ill?'

'This is getting fucking ridiculous!' she shouted. 'You're not acting like yourself. All of this stuff you keep going on about is just anxiety bullshit. You're not dying.'

'How do you know?'

The next day, I begged her to let me spend money we didn't have on a series of private ultrasound scans so I could rule out the various cancers that I was sure I had.

'And then what?' she said. 'Then, it'll be something else. For the last time: please see a therapist.'

'I don't need to. I promise you.'

65

The water was a long way down. The city lights were playing kiss chase on the water's surface. Skipping. Dancing. Skimming. Some of the prettiest reds and blues I'd ever seen. It was cold. Bitterly cold for late September. I had my hands in my pockets. A grey wool scarf tied tight around my neck. A head full of Anne Sexton's poetry. Her words had become friends. They were clearings in the chaos. Places where I didn't feel like I was losing my mind. Like I was crazy. Like I was dying. The bridge was busy with people rushing to and from the South Bank. I was on my way to see a Robert Bresson film. Anna had arranged weeks before to see a play with a friend. I was going to stay home but then I saw the film was on and decided to go. It's about a young woman who commits suicide. That got my attention. Little else did. The idea of suicide was starting to seem quite normal. Like buying a loaf of bread or going to buy a paper.

The River Thames splashed below. Black. Blue. Filthy. Dirty. Everything played out in slow motion. A blur of colours. Derailment. Slow and painful. There was a sudden whoosh in my head: a dam bursting. A giddy, hysterical flood of impulsiveness. An overwhelming hunger to throw myself off the bridge. Down into the water. There was a split-second division in my heart. I wanted to jump. I didn't want to jump. The pull was so violent, so savage, as if suicide had reached into my stomach and was dragging me by the entrails towards death. My legs readied themselves to make the leap. It all happened so fast. None of this lasted more than ten seconds. But each second was a lifetime. The rational response – you're depressed, you're not making sense, you have responsibilities to those who love you, think of Anna, think of your family – hurried me to the guard rail. I grabbed hold of the steel. I was shaking. Cold sweat. Heart palpitations. The rush-hour pedestrian flow blew through me, anonymous voices cursing me for blocking the small foot bridge from Embankment tube station over to the South Bank. I hurried across the bridge, shuffling my hands along the railing as if I was scaling a rope. When I got to the other side, I didn't know what to do with myself. I thought I'd gone crazy. I went into the cinema toilets and splashed cold water on my face. When I looked into a mirror, a stranger stared back at me. I sat in the cinema and the film began. A young woman leaped to her death. From her apartment. Many floors up. Crushed on the street below.

When I got home, I couldn't bring myself to tell Anna what had happened. I knew how much it would hurt her. And I didn't want to hurt her. I only wanted to hurt myself.

66

A week later, I finally told her what had happened – or what had almost happened – and she walked me to the medical centre. I saw another new doctor. The doctor's questions were so familiar that I almost knew every question before it came out of his mouth. He wanted to know everything: that I write for a living, that Anna and I got married in April, that we bought a flat in June, that I'd been between book contracts since May. And, of course, that I had a history of depression. And anxiety. And that I was a recovering alcoholic. I was surprised when I told him this. It was out there, free. Finally, I had told a doctor the truth. When there was nothing more to say, I was diagnosed once again as suffering from severe depression and anxiety. I was prescribed the same antidepressant as all the other times. When I got out of his room, Anna was waiting for me. I told her what he said. We were both relieved because it was over. The fighting, the running, the denial. At last, I was destroyed.

By the time it was dark, the foundations of my sober life to date were charred, smouldering, erased. I was a complete blank. Nothing meant anything except my love for Anna. After dinner, I popped a red Prothiaden pill from the blister pack into the palm of my hand. I looked at the pill. It looked at me. You again, we both whispered in unison.

67

Everything smears when I try to give that winter a narrative. There just isn't one. I remember going back to the medical centre after a fortnight and nearly breaking down in front of the doctor when he asked me how I was. I remember that he put me on the maximum dose and that, as before, it made it impossible for me to get out of bed in the mornings. I remember feeling drugged and drowsy. I remember so many appointments with the doctor. Always the same questions, the same crap, the same symptoms. Side effects like confusion, dizziness, constipation, headaches, forgetfulness. Seeing a hypnotherapist for most of December. I remember the monthly walk to the chemist's between the medical centre and home, the handing over of the prescription, the five-minute wait while the pharmacist packed a paper bag with blister packs of antidepressants. The doctors, the pills, the afternoon naps, the sleepless nights, the freezing cold mornings, that's all the winter was. A long, deafening blackout.

68

Déjà vu shadowed every step I took. When I suddenly knew where I was – a building or a bar or a subway sign triggering memories that weren't quite real – there was the sense that I had borrowed someone else's life. I'd go into bookstores that looked interesting and realise that I'd been there before. I'd go into a bar for a cold Coke and recognise the chairs, the tables, or the name of the place. We all re-write our pasts to make them manageable, bearable. During that week, back in New York for the first time in eight years, I again realised how out of control I'd once been. Holed up at Hotel 31, my brain dulled by jet lag and antidepressants, I scrutinised maps, and then set out to discover my past. I tried and failed to find the apartment building that Jennifer lived in. I didn't even know where Jennifer lived any more. Or Kristen. They were just names now. Faces that once meant something. I took Anna to a bar in the East Village, where a man once pulled a hunting knife on a friend of mine when he walked into what he thought was an empty cubicle. It was a dive, a place that gave me the creeps. We had a quick drink and left. On the streets outside, walking along the Bowery, I shivered and wondered how I'd got that fucked up.

69

Spring was in full swing. The bell jar was lifting. Seven months of pills and there was colour again. A full palette of excitement even. I went to bed at night and slept until morning. I cooked elaborate dinners. Anna and I re-decorated our flat, both of us keen to begin a new era, another chapter. Writing this book helped me start to make sense of my past. I started to understand why things happened. And how they stopped happening. And started again.

70

The sun's shining. It's a wonderful afternoon in early summer. I'm sitting in one of the finest restaurants in Paris with Roman Polanski. I've been sent to Paris to interview him. Like all my work as a journalist, I'm repaying debts to those whose work helped me through difficult times, whose giving gave me a reason to live. I ask him a question about his film *Repulsion*. When he's talking about how he directed Catherine Deneuve in a specific scene, I remember how often I referred to that film in my sessions with Veronica. I was too busy learning to open up and talk about my feelings to be able to describe them in simple terms. So I used to use scenes and characters from films to speak for me. And then I get the chills, because nine years have passed and I'm about to turn thirty and sitting at a table with a man I used to idolise. When the interview wraps up, I have him sign his autobiography for me.

Later, on a Eurostar train, coming home, I realise that I had him sign his book for the person I once was. I got that autograph for the person who used to sit in that little room with Veronica, his arms covered in cuts, a hangover chewing his liver up, depression crackling in his brain. And now . . . I just got paid to spend an afternoon with Roman Polanski. I feel so happy I want to stand up and tell the whole train. I want to time travel back to Veronica's room and give myself a big hug. I open the book as we go through the Channel Tunnel and stare at the inscription. And then I close it and smile because a beautiful woman is waiting for me at home. And I can't believe that either.

71

11 June 2000. Thirty years old. Five years and eight months sober. Anna and I are sitting in a restaurant in Paris, my favourite city in the whole world. She surprised me by booking this two-day trip as a present. She sips a glass of red wine. I sip a glass of Badoit mineral water.

Badoit: the champagne of my sobriety. What I always drink on special occasions.

'Happy thirtieth birthday,' says Anna.

She raises her glass of red wine. I raise my glass of Badoit. I am finally comfortable with the fact that I am a recovering alcoholic. We clink glasses. We did the same thing the night before for Anna's birthday.

'Guess I'm an old man now,' I say, messing around.

'Hey old man,' she replies.

We laugh.

I am always laughing with her.

I didn't laugh much before she came into my life.

'I love you.'

All of Paris is behind her, out the window, lights, people, cars, bikes.

'I love you too,' she replies. 'Remember the cards?'

Somehow, out of all the cards in the world, we bought each other the exact same birthday card.

72

There's a point with antidepressants where you hit auto-pilot. They can only take you so far. And then you walk into a haze. The kind of haze that hangs over Los Angeles early in the morning. The world is warm and fuzzy. You bump into furniture. Forget to call people back. Go out to buy a carton of milk and come home with everything but. Things get too cosy, too comfortable. Real life is so far away. The medication drives a wedge between you and the depression. And once that wedge has been created and sustained, something else is needed to scare the depression away. Therapy is the obvious answer. Exercise another.

It was Anna's idea that we both start going to a kick-boxing class. I wasn't really interested. It took a lot of persuading to get me to go. I was still having down days, days when I felt hopeless and agitated. They were happening less and less but were enough of a concern for my doctor to offer me short-term counselling. I knew we'd waste the six sessions I was allowed under NHS policy just setting the scene. So Anna dragged me to this class. I went along and it changed everything. At last, a type of exercise that got rid of all of my negative feelings. Running, swimming, cycling, those were just fads that scratched the surface. This was it. This did it.

I've gone once a week ever since. I leave those classes drenched in sweat, exhausted, everything purged. There's no one-on-one combat, it's all based on principles of shadow boxing. The class is in a gym with mirrored walls. When we kick and box, the instructor tells us to direct all of our anger at our own reflection. When I kick or punch, I am beating and pummelling the depressed me, the alcoholic me, the cutting me, the addictive me. I look at him as he stares at me, antidepressants buzzing in my veins, and I attack him with all my strength.

When every muscle is burning, aching, I am alive. When I am drenched in sweat, I like to think of the sweat as my past. I am purging memories. My body remembers everything. I have written on it. Damaged it. Abused it. Bankrupted it. Now I am paying it back. There is a debt. A debt of flesh. I throw a jab. A cross. A hook. An upper cut. I skip. Dance on my feet. Guard up. I cover my face with my fists. Lash out. Anchor my brain's lust for meandering thought. I am centred. In balance. I am in control of every breath, every punch, every kick. My mind and body are in tune. Keen collaborators. For so long they were enemies. There was war in my blood. Soul and body fought. Now they are united in a common fight: the fight for health, sobriety, strength, peace of mind.

The kick-boxing broke the deadlock of this depression. It capitalised on the work done by the antidepressants and helped push the depression away. Soon, the pounds were falling off me. I was so out of shape and overweight when I went to that first class. I had ballooned up to almost fourteen stone on the medication. Within a month, I had shed a stone. I do some kind of exercise at least every other day now. I am learning to exorcise the moods that create a perfect breeding ground for anxiety, panic attacks, depression, the craving for a drink. The goal is to learn to identify dangerous thoughts and moods and then to beat them out of me before they find a foothold.

73

I caught myself one day, as Anna and I were fooling around and said, 'I'm laughing.'

'I know,' she said. 'You're back.'

'Where did I go?'

'Palookaville.'

'Was I gone long?'

We stopped kidding around. Anna had tears in her eyes.

'A long, long time.'

I hugged her.

'You know,' I said. 'I'd die without you.'

74

It was a hot day in July. A sudden thirst stopped me in my tracks. For the first time since I quit drinking, I craved a chilled bottle of mineral water. The craving for a cold beer that popped up whenever the sun came out had finally been replaced. I'm getting there, I thought, chuckling, and strode out into the sun's rays. Warm, surprised, back from the dead.

I felt like myself again. A better version of myself. Happy even. I wasn't angry any more. I had been angry for so long. Now, I had a little peace of mind. Some balance. Some quiet. I didn't resent the depression I was almost through with. I saw it as a gift. It had just been time for me to shed another skin. That was all. Time to move forwards, come to an end, start a new beginning. A part of me died and I mourned it for a long time. And then there were things to do.

'Congratulations,' the doctor said. 'You've done so well to come out of this depression. You've fought it and you've beaten it.'

Back at the medical centre. September 2000. A year after I turned up there dreaming of going to sleep and never waking up again.

'Thank you.'

He smiled at me. We had talked over my progress. I told him that I wanted to come off the medication. We had been reducing my dose, bit by bit, down from 150mg a day to 125mg to 100mg. I'd levelled out at 75mg and wanted to drop another dose.

'Let's turn this over to you now. I'll give you a prescription that will put you on fifty milligrams for a fortnight and then twenty-five milligrams for a fortnight. You monitor how you feel. If you feel shaky come back and see me. Otherwise, I think it's time for you to come off them now.'

77

When I go down to 50mg, I instantly notice the difference. My body shrinks. I lose five pounds in the first week. I realise how much the medication has been damaging my metabolism. I have so much energy. The energy of a power station. I panic when I can't get to sleep on the first few nights. Oh, this again. The tossing and turning. The thoughts taking off and landing like planes. An airport for a brain. The creak of the bed. Anna fast asleep beside me. Wanting to get up and write. To exercise. To check e-mail. To maximise my life. Stall death. The insomnia drags on, night after night, all the way to 25mg. But the big difference this time is I don't get scared. This is real life. All over the world, there are people who can't get to sleep.

It's a regular shopping trip. I walk down to the super-market and buy some food. When I pass the alcohol aisle, a voice calls out to me.

'Would you like to try this wine, sir?'

A man is smiling at me. He is surrounded by glass. Tiny taster tumblers in front of him like babies.

'No thanks,' I call back.

'Are you sure?' he says, holding a tumbler of red wine up in the air, hoping to woo me to his station of pain.

'Yes,' I tell him. 'I am sure.'

79

A Friday night. The city's on fire. Bars. Neon Budweiser signs. People shouting. Spilling on to the streets. The giggle of ice cubes. Tears of a lime. Lemons. Cocktail menus. Beer nuts. Shots of tequila. Anna and I walk into a pub. The atmosphere makes my hair stand on end. We queue at the bar. A gin and tonic. A ginger ale. We sit and sip our drinks. Maybe my exile is over. Maybe it will never be over. I've made my peace with this drinking thing, though. Six years sober. We make a toast to the future and I get the strongest sense that everything's going to be all right.

80

Sunday 19 November 2000. I tip the last of my antide-pressants into the palm of my hand. I ended up staying on

25mg for six weeks because there was too much turbulence. I'm scared to death of coming off them. I've been taking them since September 1999. That's a long time to have something in your bloodstream. Dulling things. Calming me down. Helping me sleep. Keeping my serotonin levels in balance. I wash it down with a mug of Night Time herbal tea, close my eyes and hope.

81

Then, a year where vodka and grapefruit juice was my number-one drink.

Now, fifteen consecutive nights of eating pasta.

Then, six months bingeing on Colt 45.

Now, a year of tracking down first editions of Anne Sexton's books.

Then, two years of drinking vodka and Pernod.

Now, only buying Agnes B. shirts for a year.

Then, eighteen months of Gamay and Beaujolais.

Now, weeks learning everything there is to know about Italy.

Then, Rebel Yell on the rocks was 'my drink' for two months.

Now, almost a year of only listening to hip-hop.

I am an addict. Always will be.

82

It's almost Christmas again. I'm still kick-boxing every week. Going to yoga now too. Still working out at home whenever I can. Still taking kava kava and Nytol and valerian root and Quiet Life and zinc and magnesium and calcium and vitamin B complex and eating tryptophan rich foods like peanut butter and avocados. Still drinking Sleepytime Tea and espresso and green tea and camomile tea. Still impulsive. Still moody. Still have problems sleeping. Still have problems relaxing. Still have panic attacks. Still have days when I crave a drink. Still worry about everything. Still have days when I feel like I'm getting depressed again. Still have days when my moods are all over the place. But these things are me and always will be. I have no regrets. So many gifts. Parents who love me. A sister who loves me. A wife who loves me. This whole story, a story I'm lucky to have. The way I am, a blessing, no longer a curse. Anna and I have surprised each other by talking more and more about having a child. Bringing a little one into this life, this world.

83

Up days, down days, in-between days. Days of desperate blue. Memories. Calling me back. I have to stay strong. And furnish the rest of my life with acceptance and hope. It won't ever stop. This won't ever stop. This is me. We're in it for the long run. Me and everything inside. All sweet emotion. And bitter loss. Feelings. Beautiful blue birds. Wings beating. Skies forgiving. Happier climes. And soothing words. The orchestra is busy with love. And I want to sing. Clear and loud. Love's melody. Out of tune. Such pretty words. I wrote them for you. I wrote them all for you.

A NOTE ON THE TYPE

The text of this book is set in Linotype Sabon, named after the type founder, Jacques Sabon. It was designed by Jan Tschichold and jointly developed by Linotype, Monotype and Stempel, in response to a need for a typeface to be available in identical form for mechanical hot metal composition and hand composition using foundry type.

Tschichold based his design for Sabon roman on a fount engraved by Garamond, and Sabon italic on a fount by Granjon. It was first used in 1966 and has proved an enduring modern classic.